Also by William F. Buckley, Jr.

Editor

GRATITUDE

☆ ☆ ☆ ☆ ☆ ☆ ☆

Gratitude

★ ★ ★ ★ ★ ★ ★ ★ ★ ★ ★ ★

REFLECTIONS ON WHAT WE OWE TO OUR COUNTRY

William F. Buckley, Jr.

☆ ☆ ☆ ☆ ☆ 🏠 ☆ ☆ ☆ ☆ ☆

RANDOM HOUSE   NEW YORK

Grateful acknowledgment is made to the following for permission
to reprint previously published material:
LEXINGTON BOOKS: Excerpts from *National Service: What Would It
Mean?* by Richard Danzig and Peter Szanton (Lexington, MA:
Lexington Books, D.C. Heath & Co.) Copyright © 1987 by D.C.
Heath and Company. Reprinted by permission of the publisher.
THE NEW REPUBLIC: Excerpts from "1000 Points of Lite" by James
Bennett from the November 7, 1988, issue of *The New Republic*.
Copyright © 1988 by The New Republic, Inc. Reprinted by per-
mission of *The New Republic*.
THE WASHINGTON POST: Excerpt from "Sam Nunn Wants You" by
Michael Kinsley from the May 19, 1988, issue of *The Washington
Post*. Copyright © 1988 by *The Washington Post*. Reprinted by
permission.

Library of Congress Cataloging-in-Publication Data
Buckley, William F. (William Frank), 1925–
Gratitude/by William F. Buckley.
p. cm.
ISBN 0-394-57674-8
1. National service—United States. I. Title.
HD4870.U6B83 1990
361.6'0973—dc20   90-53126

BOOK DESIGN BY LILLY LANGOTSKY

FOR EDWARD PULLING

—TEACHER AND FRIEND, DEVOTEDLY

A C K N O W L E D G M E N T S

☆ ☆ ☆ ☆ ☆ ☆ ☆ ☆ ☆ ☆ ☆

*T*he idea of national service, however inchoate, inched into my mind and was given formal expression in a few pages of my book *Four Reforms* (1974). The idea grew (metastasized?) into this slender volume.

I am deeply indebted to Dorothy McCartney, the research director of *National Review*, for her productive and good-humored help with research. To Frances Bronson, who superintends all my editorial activity. To Tony Savage, who typed and organized the manuscript. To Chaucy Bennetts, who has once again served me so ably as copy editor. My thanks also to Olga Tarnowski, for a fine and helpful editorial reading.

And to Joseph Isola, who read the galleys with an eye sharpened by the splendid help he has given me on twenty-four of my books.

This book depends, as my last fifteen books have done, on the creative suggestions of Samuel S. Vaughan, indispensable editor, indispensable friend. And I am especially obliged to Michael Lind, a young scholar living in Washington, whom I persuaded to help me develop some of the ideas in this book. His suggestions were provocative, creative, and shrewd.

Edward Pulling, to whom the book is dedicated, founded the Millbrook School from which I graduated in 1943. He stressed, as I relate in the text, the idea of community service at his school, and I suppose that makes him the progenitive author of a book which may not suit him in detail, but which I hope he will perceive as an act of gratitude.

W.F.B.

STAMFORD, CONNECTICUT

MAY 1, 1990

C O N T E N T S

INTRODUCTION:
ON GRATITUDE

☆　☆　☆　☆　☆　☆　☆　☆　☆　☆　☆

I have always thought Anatole France's story of the juggler to be one of enduring moral resonance. This is the arresting and affecting tale of the young monk who aspires to express his devotion to the Virgin Mary, having dejectedly reviewed, during his first week as a postulant at the monastery alongside Our Lady of Sorrows, the prodigies and gifts of his fellow monks. Oh, some sang like nightingales, others played their musical instruments as virtuosi, still others rhapsodized with the tongues of poets. But all that this young novice had learned in the way of special skills before entering the monastery was to entertain modestly as a juggler. And so, in the dead of night, driven by the mandate to serve, walking furtively lest he be seen and mocked by his brothers, he makes his ardent way to the altar with his sackful of wooden mallets and balls, and does his act for Our Lady.

This account of the struggle to express gratitude is unsurpassed in devotional literature. The apparent grotesquerie—honoring the mother of the savior of the universe, the vessel of salvation, with muscular gyrations designed to capture the momentary interest of six-year-olds—is inexpressibly beautiful in the mind's eye. The act of propitiation; gratitude reified.

How to acknowledge one's devotion, one's patrimony, one's heritage? Why, one juggles before the altar of God, if that is what one knows to do. That Americans growing into citizenhood should be persuasively induced to acknowledge this patrimony and to demonstrate their gratitude for it is the thesis of this exercise. By asking them to make sacrifices we are reminding them that they owe a debt, even as the juggler felt a debt to Our Lady. And reminding them that requital of a debt is the purest form of acknowledging that debt. The mind tends to turn to the almsgiver as one experiences the alms he has to give us. We are familiar with the debt an exonerated defendant feels toward the judicial system on which he suddenly found himself relying. The man truly hungry looks with a different eye on the person who feeds him.

It is entirely possible to live out an entire life without experiencing the civic protections that can become
so contingently vital to us at vital moments. Even if
we never need the help of the courts, or of the policeman, or of the Bill of Rights, that they are there for us
in the event of need distinguishes our society from most
others. To alert us to their presence, however dormant
in our own lives, tends to ensure their survival. And
tends also to encourage a citizenry alert to the privileges the individual might one day need or enjoy. This
enjoyment, this answering of needs, can make us
proud of our country—and put us in its debt.

In this essay on the theme of Gratitude I postulate
that we do owe something. To whom? The dead being
beyond our reach, our debt can only be expressed to
one another; but our gratitude is also a form of obei-
sance—yes, to the dead.

The points I raise will disturb some "conservative"
presumptions as also some commonly thought of as
"liberal." I have, in any event, the obligation to explore
the social meaning of duty. Those who respond to religious guidelines will not be surprised by the Christian
call to reinspect divine commandments: "Verily I say
unto you, inasmuch as ye have done it unto one of the
least of these my brethren, ye have done it unto me."
Although religious faith is not required to prompt attention to the nature of the injunction, the intensity of
the concern of some Americans is sometimes best

understood by the use of religious metaphors. Emil Durkheim wrote engrossingly on the question when he spoke of the "relation of a devoted child to his parents, of an ardent patriot to his fatherland, [of a] cosmopolitan to mankind, of a worker to his class, of a nobleman conscious of his rank to the aristocracy, of the vanquished to his conqueror, of the good soldier to his army." "All these relations," Durkheim concluded, "with their infinitely manifold contents can, indeed do, have a general tenor as far as their psychic aspect is concerned—which must be called a religious key."

Durkheim might have added to his list the relation of the citizen to the community organized to protect his rights: an intensity which can be called religious characterizes the devotion shown to their community by literally millions of people who routinely sacrifice— time, money, labor—to remark that devotion; and, using their own methods, skills, and language, to requite the community. Mother Teresa characterizes her altruistic, prodigious efforts as an attempt to repay the Lord for bringing her to life, and giving her an opportunity for perpetual life by His side. The anonymous soldier who volunteers for a dangerous mission to enhance the prospects of the army that seeks to defend his nation is moved by a great passion to serve. Most service isn't heroic in character—they also serve who only stand and wait. But service is twice ennobling: it acknowledges that which deserves veneration, and satisfies the hunger of those who cannot be satisfied save by a gesture of requital. That as a nation we should encourage the requital of such young citizens is the enthusiastic premise of these pages.

Coming very slowly to a boil in Congress is the question of national service. It is a very old idea, by the way. George Washington spoke in favor of national service, which was commonly supposed at the time to be service in the military, it being military preparedness that was in those days most commonly needed to defend against the agents of His Majesty King George, or the red-skinned agents of Chief Charging Bull. The proposition that American citizens owe something to the community that formulated and fought to establish their progenitive rights was proffered in 1910 by William James, in an essay still widely referred to as a kind of charter instrument of national service ("The Moral Equivalent of War"). The durability of the idea of national service at the very least betokens an inherent appeal. It was all so very much easier to speak about, and even to fancy, back when the tradition of public service meant the military. The Ferocity of the Warrior was readily transmuted to The Pride of the Father. In an age in which military contention absorbs less and less social energy (it has been seventeen years since an American was drafted for military duty), the eye roams, under the prompting of a parched heart, for service of another kind; for the satisfaction, say, of juggling for Our Lady.

Both political parties, since the presidential contest of 1988, have declared themselves in favor of national service. Indeed, Democratic Senator Sam Nunn, acting for his party, introduced as the very first bill (S.3) in January 1989 a Citizenship and National Service Bill. What it says, to use only a few words to describe it, is that young people should be induced to give service to the nation. By no means does the bill propose that national service be limited to the military. Indeed, since the bill was introduced, because of the happy events of 1989 in the communist bloc it becomes apparent that we face the need for fewer, rather than for more, soldiers in the field. Accordingly, the efforts of many national service volunteers would be directed to extra-military pursuits, of which there are a dismaying number. Dismaying in this sense: if you add up the number of young people whose services could profitably be used in helping old people; in assisting teachers both in instructing children and in protecting them; in advancing environmental goals; in protecting deteriorating books in libraries, say, you add up quickly to more than one half of the three million Americans who, every year, become eighteen years old. The Nunn bill addresses the younger generation and says, Look, if you will agree to give us a year of your time in national service, we will pay you ten thousand dollars

beyond the pocket money you will get during your
national service. This ten thousand dollars you can use
toward your college tuition payments, if you go on to
college; or as a down payment on your mortgage when
you get around to buying a house. It is conceived as a
grand federal enterprise, and I do not wish only for
that reason to oppose it, though I do so for reasons I
will elaborate.

As of this writing, the Republicans have (I con-
cede, as I'll do later in greater detail) a halfhearted
substitute bill, not worth exploring. It is very much
worth remarking, however, that the subject of national
service, although the debate about it has not yet
reached the voter's hearth, is very much there, a subject
waiting to be deliberated. It is going to run into any
number of hostile presumptions, among them the
aversion to an idea of federally sponsored philanthropy
(though the federal government has long since en-
couraged philanthropy by granting tax deductions); an
egalitarian resistance to special favors for special
classes of citizens (though the government has long
since favored veterans with the G.I. Bill, which pays
much of college educational costs); and, not least, the
inertial resistance to the blight of any Grand New National Idea. I hope to confront these objections, and
even to suggest that every conceivable Grand New National Idea ought not to be discarded out of hand.
(Wouldn't many of us agree that it would be a Grand

New National Idea to replace "The Star-Spangled Banner" with "America the Beautiful"?)

Meanwhile, it is fair to note that those politicians who have entered into the argument, and they are both Democrats and Republicans, are saying that participation in the community should take more active form than merely paying taxes, buying and selling in the marketplace, and voting (occasionally, if at all). And of course the question is necessarily raised in context of the one question we can never get away from. I treasure the story of Congressman Rich of Pennsylvania, who sat in the House of Representatives for years and years and rose to speak in session after session, year after year, to make only the one simple comment before sitting down again: "How are we going to pay for all this?" And then one day, at two o'clock in the morning, after the House had been in session continuously for over two days and a bleary quorum was ready for the final vote—up shot the hand of Congressman Rich, resignedly acknowledged by the Speaker, to a chorus of vocal dismay. He rose and said solemnly, "April Fool!"

Even on April 1, the question of cost cannot be dismissed. I reveal at this early moment that I deem it entirely manageable. But just as the question is bound to arise—how much will National Service cost?—so an advocate of the idea is required to consider that cost and to explore its ramifications. In the

last analysis a society *has* to accumulate a surplus before it gets around to thinking in terms of expenditures
beyond those absolutely necessary to produce food and
shelter. Without an economic surplus we are left with
not even enough to afford a set of the juggler's mallets
and balls.

Of course. Practical attention needs to be paid to
the question of national service, but if the idea takes
over the public imagination, as it has done my own,
the cost will prove bearable, and its fruits beyond the
reach of slide rules. And then, properly conceived, the
status of the citizen in a republic, uniting privilege with
responsibility, evolves into a kind of nobility no less
aristocratic for being widespread and universally ac-
cessible (is there any difficulty in conceiving of a society, every one of whose members is of an aristocratic
order?). Materialistic democracy beckons every man
to make himself a king; republican citizenship incites
every man to be a knight. National service, like gravity,
is something we could accustom ourselves to, and grow
to love.

Gratitude

★ ★ ★ ★ ★ ★ ★ ★ ★ ★ ★

REFLECTIONS ON WHAT
WE OWE TO OUR COUNTRY

☆   ☆   ☆   ☆   ☆   ☆   ☆   ☆   ☆   ☆   ☆

Robert Ely

*L*et us imagine a personal experience, occurring a few years down the line. And let us think of normal human beings, here defined as unlikely to become stars of Hollywood, television, Congress, or Skid Row. I think of Robert Ely as a human being who might, or might not, personally engage me; certainly he would not repel me. He is Mr. Young Citizen, the kind of person who has engrossed the attention of sociologists from Staughton Lynd to Studs Terkel. Is the following narrative—carefully, scrupulously deglamorized—plausible?

Robert Ely graduated from high school while still a month or two short of his eighteenth birthday. Accepted by two of the five colleges he had applied to, he decided on the University of Connecticut, where he would study business administration. The tuition, even at a state college, presented a problem, but not, he calculated, an insuperable problem. He would qualify for a modest scholarship, and would work part-time during the school semesters and full-time during the summer vacations. Under the new legislation he wouldn't qualify, unless he served in National Service, for a federal loan, notwithstanding that his father, a postal worker invalided in his early fifties, had only his pension to rely on, supplemented by his mother's relatively modest contribution to the joint exchequer— her salary as a receptionist at a local clinic. And they had to bear the expenses of Robert's younger sister, Susan. He would need to think about it.

His parents were united in associating themselves enthusiastically with the trend that had been crystallizing during the early 1990s, and though it would have suited everyone's convenience to get on with Robert's education, he was reconciled to a year's national service.

It had been a subject of endless discussion at his high school, 85 percent of whose seniors went on to college. Only five years earlier, a mere 10 percent of the graduating class had submitted to the year's delay in their education that National Service entailed. But that 10 percent—eight boys, six girls—were specially recognized at graduation as having accepted a challenge, the allure of which had grown keener in the interval leading to Robert's own graduation. The year before, the figure had been not 10 percent of his class, but more nearly 50 percent. That one half who did not sign up for National Service were articulate about their reasons.

One senior, Mark Hemmelrich, said that he absolutely had to matriculate this coming September at the University of Arizona because he had been awarded the annual scholarship available to aspiring botanists and there was no way of knowing whether, in the succeeding year, engaging in the same competition, he would prevail against that season's entries.

Kathy Ellis's pregnancy had become all too obvious, as had, by implication, her decision not to abort her child. She spoke bluntly when the subject was raised: She had made a mistake, she was going to bear her child and could hardly consider simultaneous altruism in behalf of others. Leave her alone, please.

Isabelle Noyes said she could not possibly put off her college education for an entire year, given that her mother's deteriorating health made it imperative that someone take on the job of bookkeeping for her father, an optician, a few years hence. The strain on her mother's weak constitution was palpable and there wouldn't be enough income to pay for a professional bookkeeper when her mother's health finally broke down—obviously, she explained, her first duty was to her own family; she must get on, without delay, with college.

Josh Minelli was also outspoken. His prowess in basketball had brought to town several coaches from colleges with prominent teams and there was no way he could be persuaded to end the bidding match for him by announcing that he was going to take a year off "to teach dunk shots to the Patagonians," as he put it. He did not welcome extended analysis of his alternatives.

Robert recognized that others had rather compelling reasons for foregoing National Service. And if things had been as they were during his freshman year, Robert mused, he might have beaten back the pressure to "do the National Service thing," as his classmates had regularly referred to it, though the phrase was nowadays less widely used.

But not now, he reflected. It wasn't merely that he didn't have a compelling excuse—oh, he was ingenious enough to contrive *something*, certainly something more plausible than Al Trimble's excuse. (Al was an ostentatious votary of astrology, and would explain to anyone at all who inquired why, for a Sagittarius born in 1976, matriculating at college this year, 1994,

wasn't a matter of choice, it was *ordained!*) The trouble
was, Robert couldn't persuade himself to look very
hard for an excuse.

Robert's aunt, as it happened, had recently
moved—or rather had been moved from the little
apartment she shared with her sister-in-law to an old
people's home. Robert had always been fond of Aunt
Lucy but when Aunt Lucy's problem was explained to
him, using the lace-curtain language common when
talking about certain maladies, Robert said that he
understood, and when the appointed day came to move
her and her few possessions, Robert was there with the
old family station wagon to lend a hand. Taking her
from the car to the institutional elevator of Owlwood
Retirement Home, he found he was being helped by
a young man approximately his own age on whose
hospital smock he spotted the little red knit, telltale,
emblem "NS."

Might they have a cup of coffee together, Robert
asked, after Aunt Lucy had been settled down? The
young man looked down at his watch. "It's 11:10. If
you want to wait until noon, sure; but I'm not free until
then." Robert agreed, and the young orderly—his
name was Carl Pepper—indicated where in the caf-
eteria they would meet.

They had lunch, Carl paying for his corned beef
sandwich and soup with coupons he drew from his

pocket. It transpired that Carl had been at the hospital nine months and would finish his NS in time to go to college in the fall.

"Can you tell me about it?"

Yes, Carl said, he could. It was a lot of work. Twelve hours on duty every other day, which clocked in at forty-two hours per week. Tough—but still, Carl said, his view of old people was now . . . different. He had known a lot of old people—his great-grandmother was still alive, as a matter of fact. "But here I see them old and also disabled. I have seen a lot of people, I mean *a whole lot of people* . . . well, die." He spoke of one old man who had told Carl—"in just as many words, I mean that is *exactly* how he said it, he said, one afternoon, 'Carl, I am going to die between midnight and one in the morning, and you go off duty at midnight, but I would like you with me. I want to be looking at you when I die."

Well, said Carl, what alternative did he have, under the circumstances? So he stayed on, and at exactly 12:45 "Mr. Muzzio looked at me and smiled just a little, and said, 'This is it'—and, I don't kid you, he just stopped breathing. I did the usual things, felt his pulse and so on, and yes, he was dead. If you can't stand to see people die, better go somewhere else."

Robert left after lunch but only after picking up some leaflets about Owlwood Retirement Home which, Carl said, went into "a whole lot of detail but it's, you know, like reading about a school or a college. You never really find out about it until you go there."

"What exactly is it you've found out?" Robert wanted to know.

"Oh . . . a lot," said Carl, getting up from the lunch table.

aesthetic. One correctly *struggles* to distinguish between reveling in the *Passion* and rejoicing in it,
because the latter sensation awakens an extrapersonal
sense of obligation for the pleasures received.

Or consider the Oxford English Dictionary. It is
sensually pleasurable even to write about *that* mira-
cle—not simply the dictionary, but its astonishing new
accessibility, the lexicographical equivalent of the *Passion* on compact disks. It is expensive today, but will
be less so tomorrow, I warrant; currently the whole of
the O.E.D. (the original edition) can be had for nine
hundred and fifty dollars on a single disk. This ac-
complishment permits you not merely to avoid the in-
dignity of picking up a volume and hunting down the
word you are looking for, but to mobilize disparate
energies of an entirely different kind in order to pursue
allied or entirely different interests. You can ask your
computer etymological questions, or historical and literary questions, causing it to dispatch millions of bytes
of energy to scurry about several million words in order
to assemble, in any sequence that suits your curiosity,
and present to you, neatly collated, anything you wish
to put together that lies within the pages of the
dictionary. (How long would it take you, manually, to
establish how frequently citations from the book of
Isaiah had been used?) How do you "repay" the debt
one has to those mostly anonymous lexicographers
who labored, and indeed continue to do so, to give us,

at the touch of a finger, access to information elec-
tronically delivered that a battalion of monks working
several lifetimes could not accumulate?

Access. Freedom. I think back to an afternoon in
1955 when I visited the University of Salamanca and
was taken to its original library. Salamanca is the second oldest university in Europe and in one of its rooms,
not much larger than a barbershop, reposes the entire
known literature of the West, as of the thirteenth century. The scholars and the monks could enter the library to do their studying. But a Big Bertha was there,
a really big cannon to discourage them from removing
from that little room any of its all but irreplaceable
treasures. The ultimate weapon continues to hang over
the arched doorway, a few lines of calligraphy, modestly framed. *A bull of excommunication, signed by Pope
Gregory IX.* Remove a book from that library, and you
go to hell.

It goes on. I am a sailor who does his own navi-
gation. Stored inside a two-hundred-dollar instrument
about the size of my hand I have the exact geographical
location of fifty-seven navigational stars, six planets,
the sun, and the moon, for every second of every day
between now and 2010. This instrument isn't, for me,
a toy. By consulting it I have known how slightly to
nudge the wheel of my sailing vessel to come upon
remote little islands in obscure parts of the world. The
market answer to the question, How do I repay those

who made this possible? is easy: I pay the merchandiser two hundred dollars.

I am less than satisfied that I have requited that debt. Or perhaps the point is that I ought to be less than satisfied.

Yes, there are the utilitarians who will tell you that we owe nothing at all beyond whatever it is we are ready to give, in exchange for what we see displayed in the market. In a biography of Salvador Dali it is somewhere recorded that, quarreling with his father when a young man, the hot-blooded artist set out in a fury to dispose once and for all of the question, "What do I owe my father?" He sought to answer the question by withdrawing during a night of passion and sending his ejaculate to his father in an envelope marked *Paid in Full.* That was a high-wire act of reductionism, but philosophically bulletproof: The debt to one's father, repaid by the biological reciprocal. In the implicit social philosophy of too many of our contemporaries one finds little that helps to explain why this is less than an appropriate, let alone tasteful, return: this discharge of one's total obligation to one's father.

No fatherhood, no brotherhood was Nelson Rockefeller's social philosophy (as he expressed it in public. Some called it BOMFOG—the Brotherhood of Man, the Fatherhood of God). Other attempts to express collateral relations in the shared patrimony are found here and there. Tocqueville lamented that while "aristocracy had made a chain of all the members of the community, from the peasant to the king . . . democracy breaks that chain and severs every link of it. Thus, not only does democracy induce to make every man forget his ancestors, it hides his descendants and separates his contemporaries from him; it throws him back forever upon himself alone, and threatens in the end to confine him utterly within the solitude of his own heart." An arresting indictment of a democratic peril: That which makes a man a stranger to his father makes him also a stranger to his brother . . . and what severs the cords binding the generations also snaps the web that unites contemporaries.

The orphan. Solitary, estranged from tradition and therefore from communion: he is the figure of modern alienation, the making of the mass-man. Ortega y Gasset anatomized this avatar of modernity. Two decades ago I set out to write a book to remark the thirty-fifth anniversary of the appearance of his classic. I intended to call my little book "The Revolt Against the Masses," because I thought I saw on the social horizon in America signs of a disposition to reject the nescient aimlessness Ortega had diagnosed. The antinomian explosion that followed—we speak sometimes of the "Vietnam years," sometimes of the "kid years," or, simply, of "the sixties"—proved I had profoundly misread the auguries.

Ortega's analysis of the mass-man, in the rubble of the ensuing social explosion, is timelier today than when he wrote it, or when I first thought to respond. I very much wish that the meaning of the word "masses" was not so fixed in the Anglo-Saxon world as the aptest word to describe what Ortega was declaiming against, because the word as we use it has either Marxist or plutocratic connotations. True, the "masses" about which Marx wrote weren't the huddled masses welcomed by the Statue of Liberty: the masses of Emma Lazarus were merely the numerous poor. The masses of Marx were the proletariat, the hollow men of the Industrial Revolution.

Not Ortega's masses. Ortega was talking about a quality of mind unrelated to factors of wealth or poverty—or, indeed, of erudition. He was talking about the disposition of modern man *to take for granted* everything he enjoys, without any sense of incurring an obligation, either to repay the old woman from whose larder he has helped himself, or even to share with others what the larder contains.

A handy analogue is the challenge of conservation. The insight has gradually crystallized in the common consciousness that a man who cuts down a tree owes the planet one (1) seedling. In the first decades of the twentieth century, that obligation was institutionalized in the United States by various laws generally associated with the presidency of Theodore

Roosevelt. The question became subtler as, with more
polished instruments at hand, we developed skills to
measure more impalpable abrasions against the planet
than the missing tree. We began to ponder endangered
species. And the finite supply of fossil fuels. And then
the invisible particulates that attack the human lung
and the ozone layer over the earth.

About our debt to the planet there is nowadays a
considerable consciousness. A thriving social movement is concerned with conservation in the widest
sense. As with almost every movement, there are advocates who go to extremes. (Admire as I did President
Kennedy's Secretary of the Interior, Stewart Udall, I
remember writing at the high tide of his influence that
Mr. Udall sometimes left the impression that he would
have arrested the development of the West rather than
risk getting in the way of one meandering buffalo.) But
forget fanaticism: the consolidation of a social insight
is what matters.

In politics and social philosophy there is a movement which shares with conservation an etymology
that is also a perception. This perception is that the
past is alive in the present, and that all the effects of
action and thought are amplified by concentric rings
of consequence which the utilitarian's Benthamite cal-
culus are too crude to record. The movement, in politics, that has ramified from that radical perception is,
I maintain, conservatism. The conservative movement

perceives connections between the individual and the community beyond those that relate either to the state or to the marketplace. That is the point, the primary rationale, of this essay. And one need not be a conservative in other particulars to respect it.

It was this essentially conservative insight that the liberal John Stuart Mill expressed when he wrote that "though society is not founded on a contract, and though no good purpose is answered by inventing a contract in order to deduce social obligations from it, every one who receives the protection of society owes a return for the benefit, and the fact of living in a society renders it indispensable that each should be bound to observe a certain line of conduct toward the rest."

The difficulty lies in defining the appropriate "return" for the benefits. That we should answer a formal call to arms when the state is in danger is all but universally acknowledged as one of those "returns" we owe to society. A second "return" is taxation. And the nexus between that which absorbs the largest single slice of our taxes (education) and the return we are giving society raises militantly relevant questions. If a citizen is expressing a "return" to his society by consenting to be taxed for the purpose of providing education, he is presumed to care that society's children are taught and to care what it is that the society's children are going to be taught. His concern is that the children will be taught to understand the philosophical reasoning by which that seasoned citizen was himself governed years ago when he made no objection to the draft that called him to military service, and is today when he makes no objection to the tax collector who comes to get from him his share of the cost of running the schools. The schools, then, become vessels for preserving the principles that generated the disposition to sacrifice in order to make this "return" to society.

What preserves the idea beyond mere schooling? A formal attempt of requital, the citizen to the nation. The new challenge is to suggest an appropriate form, one that doesn't violate the libertarian presumption against rendering to Caesar any power Caesar does not need, and in any case ought not to want. We need to seek out the form, and to frame a policy whose ground is sunk deep in the ethos. If we succeed, democratic legitimacy comes with progressive public acceptance. This acceptance one can anticipate as the fruits of that policy become palpable and the sense of duty in the citizen is stimulated, evolving in a sense of gratitude, and is fulfilled. The citizen serene as the debtor returning from the lending institution, canceled mortgage in hand.

☆ ☆ ☆ ☆ ☆ ☆ ☆ ☆ ☆ ☆ ☆

On Changing the National Ethos

*N*ational service?

The term is loosely used, to cover at one end conscription for military or even social service, at another end, episodic attention to civic needs. What we have in mind is a program that seeks to meet needs undefined, or ill-defined, by the market, while inculcating a prime sense of citizenship among participants.

Existing attitudes in respect of national service are tantalizing. A majority (72.8 percent) of Americans "favor" national service, but a poll asking how many would support it if it involved a 5 percent increase in

their income tax tells us that enthusiasm for national
service is tenuous, dropping as it then does to 44 percent. Given that the idea, while popular, tends to be
only superficially so, it could be best described as an
idea concerning the true implications of which too few
are distinctly aware, starting with an awareness that
there is something absent from the national life—
something which wouldn't, however, be missing if the
56 percent were made aware of what is lost by its
absence, and helped to become aware of what might
be gained from its introduction.

The idea of national service needs to be pop-
ularized. Its advocates are around, here and there.
Some of them are highly mobilized (one thinks of Professor Charles Moskos of Northwestern, who is the
principal author of Senator Nunn's bill). There is the
Greek chorus of enthusiasts for any proposal that tends
to federalize human concerns—of course. But there
are also legislators who believe they understand that
out there is a hunger for concrete service. Young people
of student age with whom I have had direct experience
are divided. They are among the most idealistic of
citizens, a nice impulse of age; yet they understand
that national service is talking about *them*. It is im-
pressionistic to say they are divided, and I do not have
a statistic to suggest the size of the affirmative, over
against the negative, ranks. That the idea appeals to

the majority of Americans *is* a national statistic. That it is not (yet) a deeply felt desire is suggested by the qualification given above.

The advocates of national service believe that a growing majority of Americans show at least early signs of engagement with the idea. It is possible that the general public, apparently already on the way, will someday soon reach the point where they are resolutely behind the idea. If that were to happen, one might anticipate a day when, notwithstanding that national service continued to be voluntary, the sense of duty to volunteer would be felt by the typical citizen as keenly as, say, most young men felt a call to duty on December 7, 1941.

How do we move society in that self-protective direction, if the objective is that the Few who now believe determinedly in national service should become the Many, for whom national service is a only a velleity?

If we are engaged in promoting national service, we are engaged in the subtle business of trying to shape the national ethos. Somewhere along the line I have written that in my lifetime I have detected only two sea changes in national attitudes, one of them on a lesser scale, the second on a larger scale. The first has to do with the environment, the second with racial toleration.

Twenty-five years ago it would not have occurred to any of the hundred or so men and women I had sailed with in the preceding years to dispose of a sailboat's garbage other than by simply dumping it in the waters we cruised about in, whether Long Island Sound, Chesapeake Bay, Biscayne Bay, or the Atlantic corridor leading to Bermuda.

Today it is virtually unthinkable that any crew member would dump refuse into the water, except perhaps when a hundred miles out to sea. And even then, special care is generally taken in handling plastic bottles, whether beer bottles or Coca-Cola bottles—they are punctured, to ensure that they dribble down to the sea bed rather than float about, making their way back to the beaches.

During the fifties, and intensifying in the sixties, a sensitivity to nature was actively cultivated. The Sierra Club and its epigones, by the use of imaginatively pictured nightmares of a gutted planet—pictures given graphic life by documentaries and magazine exposés of areas of the world in which species ran the danger of extinction, in which the topsoil was eroding and rain forests disappeared—made their mark. The horror of bearing the responsibility for ushering in, however passively, a despoiled planet took a quite general hold on the imagination of men and women in America who are sensitive to ecological ethics. The point is that the number of those who were influenced greatly increased, and that this was done as a result of energetic efforts by, so to speak, lobbyists for a healthy planet.

A second change has to do with what, in any case, one might have called workaday anti-Semitism, now virtually eradicated or vastly diminished. No doubt the most immediate cause of this sea change was the Holocaust. I remember a perfect expression of what I am talking about. It was a private lunch. A distinguished public figure remarked casually that he would today leave the table in protest if he heard spoken such animadversions on the Jews as were routinely spoken at his father's table when he was a boy. The change doesn't mean (no change ever will) the end of ethnic-oriented derisive humor, even though much of it is self-consciously surreptitious in tone. It means merely that there is general acquiescence in the proposition that indifference to the rights of minorities can mutate, and during this century has done so, to genocide. National service has something in common with a sense of the intangible, but nevertheless substantial, benefits to the community that result from a lessening of the strain of social pollution which is racism.

The case for national service isn't made as neatly as the case for reclaiming the waters of Lake Erie, or of ending the quota system of college admissions. This is so because the objectives aren't in the same sense palpable (one can *see* the dirty lake, or the smog-filled

air; it isn't palpable what percentage of the freshman
class is Catholic, or, even, black; one can't "see" an
elevated national morale). We need to face the negative case for national service too—by reasoned argument, pressing the point that the *failure* to express
gratitude through disinterested social exertion brings
on the coarsening of the sensibilities, a drying out of
the wellsprings of civic and personal virtue. It isn't
easily denied that the giver is beholden—or that the
giver usually receives. It is a pity that the goo-gooism
of the political twenties (that was the term used for the
politics of a rather undifferentiated, self-advertising
civic altruism), which evolved into the feverish search
for social projects to which society might commit itself,
has done so much to disparage the politics of the
Bleeding Heart. Many Americans are put off by mac-
rocosmic projects which, subjected to hard review,
seem to have done more to sustain the bureaucratic
than the afflicted class. Many Americans are skeptical
of politically managed meliorism, as they see themselves surrounded by intensifying illiteracy, amorality,
and anomie. The lessons of misspent federal philanthropy are absolutely vital when considering national
service. But they do not and never can undermine the
absolutely secure conviction that the man or woman
who helps someone who needs help is better off for
the experience. National service is not going to satisfy
unless there is that residual tactile sense of having done

something, for somebody or some thing. As I shall later stress, my fascination with the idea of national service derives more from my anxiety that the giver receive satisfaction than that the object of his concern receive it: happily, the two are likely to go hand in hand.

In any event: To stimulate the civic ethos is the challenge, and it is plausible to adduce every argument for doing so, including the very real threat of an erosion of national morale. And, perforce, we look about us, pondering the role that national service, in whatever form, plays elsewhere.

In Switzerland there is national service. It *is* compulsory, and it is has been universally approved—the anomalous vote in the fall of 1989, which registered only 62 percent approval, notwithstanding—by a citizenry convinced that the immunity from invasion that Switzerland has enjoyed since the time of Napoleon has been the result of an ongoing national effort to make Switzerland convertible, on a moment's notice, into a steel porcupine. This shared experience in the military has unquestionably contributed to the morale of a heterogeneous nation many of whose citizens cannot speak to each other because there is no common tongue, and whose twenty-six cantons exercise a degree of independence American states haven't known since the Articles of Confederation. Switzerland is at once the least politicized and the most cohesive polit-

ical state in the West. As a regular resident of that
country for thirty years (during February and March),
I have amused myself by asking disingenuously of the
first Swiss I find myself seated next to at dinner, "Oh,
forgive me. What *is* the name of the President of Switzerland?" No one has yet been able to answer that question extemporaneously, such is the relative success of
the Swiss in republicanizing the central government.
That is the ultimate sign of national self-confidence,
surely: not bothering to know the identity of the chief
of state, the Commander in Chief.

Yes, in Switzerland the explicit focus is on military
impregnability. The strategic design—or, better, the
tactical design—is to make the conquest of Switzerland
quite simply unappetizing to the season's European
aggressor, on the grounds that to swallow Switzerland
would be on the order of, yes, swallowing a porcupine. Switzerland's National Service has nothing consciously to do with attacking poverty or illiteracy or
unemployment or helping the aged. And of course
there are the significant cultural and demographic differences: Switzerland does not welcome the huddled
masses, has no notable minority problem notwithstanding its own ethnic pluralism; and, in Switzerland,
there is no national service for women, who are not
expected to perform military service—but then, in
Switzerland the vote was only recently given to women,
and one or two cantons still hold back. That Swiss

conscription is an obligation only of men makes it even less directly relevant as a model for a voluntary civilian program of national service open to young Americans of both sexes. But the idea of a burden shared sticks in the mind, perhaps because the absence of the son, the spouse, and the father can never mean that the sacrifice is other than one shared by the mother, the wife, and the daughter; so that national military service in Switzerland is in that aspect a genuinely *national* act of civic subscription.

As it stands, National Service cultivates an intuitive recognition that every Swiss (man) "owes" something to his country; a recognition that the great legacy of Switzerland—the oldest democracy in the world, an aerie in Europe that hasn't suffered military aggression since before our Civil War—requires, oddly, constant vigilance. The long Swiss service (seventeen weeks followed by three weeks every year for eight years; followed by two weeks every year for three years, until the age of forty-two; and then two weeks once during the following eight years) is a way of reminding the citizenry that every man needs to make a sacrifice beyond paying taxes to maintain the military.

Something keeps that remarkable republic of disparate race, language, and religion together. Suppose that, next year, the Swiss government suddenly eliminated the requirement of annual service by men older than twenty-one. And that the following year the gov-

ernment eliminated altogether compulsory military
service. And, the year after, abandoned their immi-
gration laws, going on to eliminate all practical distinctions between Swiss and foreign citizenship. Before
you know it, German-speaking Switzerland is attempt-
ing to impose penalties on the French-speaking Swiss,
who doggedly retaliate in kind. And by the turn of the
century the incredible has happened: Switzerland has
become a modern Lebanon, torn by civil strife, ter-
rorism, anarchy. Looking down on Helvetia the Swiss
grandfather might indeed say ruefully to his wife, "Do
you remember the day they abandoned compulsory
military service?"

To emulate the Swiss example in the United States
would be foolish. We do not need a universal military
draft. We do need a basket of other services, which
could absorb the civic energies, were they proffered,
of three-plus million Americans, which energies are
otherwise at best dissipated, or worse, channeled into
activity hostile to home and to the community—drugs,
licentious sex, crime. Indeed, military service, for reasons advanced later, ought not to be confused with
national service, let alone serve as a substitute.

So, the Swiss example helps us only to acknowledge that one singularly successful republic, in its own
singular way, has developed an institution that certainly does one thing. It gives that republic relative
military invincibility. But something quite other, it can

be plausibly argued, developed: a national cohesion. A sense of civic responsibility. A constant reminder of the need to make sacrifices. A national morale at home reaching as high as the Alps. We learn not from their specific practice, but from the phenomenon, which yields its citizens a sense of satisfaction that comes to those who appease a hunger to requite to the land that nurtured them a measure of the profit they take from life in their land, and the land of their forebears.

☆ ☆ ☆ ☆ ☆ ☆ ☆ ☆ ☆ ☆ ☆

Anticipating the
Libertarian Argument

*W*e revisit Robert Ely, a few years
later. . . .

*It turned out to be so with Robert
Ely, that, as Carl had put it, he would find "plenty" to
think about if he signed up for his year's National Service; which he proceeded to do some days after his meet-
ing with Carl. He petitioned for service at Owlwood,
which request was granted.*

Among those he did see die, ultimately, was his
Aunt Lucy, who had suffered greatly and was much
affected by occasional contact with her great-nephew.
He lived at home, and on that account was relatively

well off because the National Service paid him one hundred dollars every week. He was qualifying for student loans while at college, and they would make just that critical difference he had at one point fretted over. And the ten-thousand-dollar tax rebate, "the G.I. Bill of National Service," as it was commonly referred to, would help him in the early years of his professional life.

He had not needed to borrow from others, after he started college, and when in junior year he decided that he would specialize in the economics of public health, he did so with a sense that he had an inside knowledge of the special problems of older people. When, four years after he was graduated, his son was born, the godmother he chose was the matron of the wing Aunt Lucy had lived in at Owlwood. The matron—Miss Effie, everybody called her—was happy to be of service to Robert and his wife, Helen, and the baby. She had stayed in touch with Robert during his college years and had twice persuaded him to give the annual introductory speech to incoming National Service volunteers. By now there were thirty-six of them at the Owlwood complex. Robert was not a public speaker. He studiously avoided any activity that might call on him to stand up and address a group of people. But for Miss Effie he would make the exception—and, it turned out, he hadn't minded talking out loud about the year he had spent "doing the NS thing, as we used

to say at school." He said that the year had changed
him. Of course, he had been asked (this was inevitable)
just *how* had it changed him? The first time he heard
the question he replied that he couldn't say. But when
Miss Effie called on him the second year, he felt that
since the question would inevitably come up again,
this time he would give some thought to how to answer
it.

So he did, and what he said when the question
was asked was that he felt he had been "changed" in
that he hadn't, at high school age, given any thought
at all to "just helping people." Now he felt he had
helped "quite a few people" in "little ways," without
hurting himself—the time spent, as he thought back
on it, had gone by quickly, "almost like a flash, if you
know what I mean." And then he said that, as he
reflected on it, he himself had been helpless for a while,
as an infant—"as all of you in this room were"—and
somebody had looked after him, and now he and his
wife were looking after their own little child, but sometime in the future—"way down the line, I hope!"—he
would be helpless again, and he liked the idea that
somebody might be around to volunteer to help him.
And besides, he said, he'd be around "on planet
Earth" a few years longer than his Aunt Lucy was, at
the going actuarial projection—maybe four or five
years longer, and since he "liked life," he figured he
owed it to somebody to say, Well, thanks for making

a longer life "a little more bearable," and so he just plain "felt better" about the whole deal.

And yes, he didn't need to tell them that qualifying for the federal college loan had helped during the college years, so it hadn't been 100 percent, well, "charity, or whatever you want to call it" on his part. But he was, yes, "glad" he had done it. "Grateful, in a way."

So. If it is all so neat—Aunt Lucy *et al.* get their young helpers, the young helpers' way through college and early life is eased financially—there is manifest satisfaction all the way around. Why doesn't the market marshal the arrangements that move us in such harmony to such ends?

This is one of the difficulties that get in the way of national service. In a price system economy, demand and supply make contact via the medium of the dollar. If one thousand children per year develop poison ivy and that affliction is treatable by one thousand bottles of calamine lotion, then entrepreneurs will foregather, on news of the outbreak of the poison ivy plague, prepared to produce one thousand bottles of calamine lotion. But in order to generate an economic demand for one thousand bottles of lotion, that demand needs, as the economists put it, to evolve as a "felt" demand. That is to say, there must be enough disposable money out there that parents of the afflicted children are prepared to exchange for a bottle of the lotion. If one hundred parents do not have the disposable surplus or, having it, choose not to spend it on calamine, then either one hundred children will do without calamine lotion, or else the money to buy the extra one hundred bottles will need to come in from another source: maybe a Children's Aid Society, spotting the suppurating victims of the untreated poison ivy, came in with the calamine. Who knows, the state may have added the care of poison ivy to its catalogue of official concerns. In any event, unless there is money to generate the calamine lotion, the children will do without.

The problem that most concerns analysts of free market disposition (I am one) has to do with the means by which society establishes the value of the kind of service we are talking about. "Value," in ordinary circumstances, is best established by the unhampered probings of the marketplace. But we are here considering injecting into the marketplace an artificial enhancement of supply, intending to meet a demand which, in orthodox economic terms, is not a "felt" demand—i.e., one that can generate its own supply by reaching out and paying for it.

Individual economic analysts might be prompted to buy or sell on the basis of their own projections about the state of the national morale, from which they will reckon productivity and competitive performance.

If they are relatively unanimous in their judgment, their collective decisions, combined with those of foreign investors, will affect the economy. But the market cannot, using its own resources, redress an ailing situation whose afflictions are not registered in conventional demand-supply terms.

Demoralizations, for example, come in many forms. A nation can become fatigued by endemic problems—major, to be sure: if the nation is constantly at war, or subject to plagues and starvation, national torpor threatens to set in. But minor—in the sense of less conspicuous—problems must be thought of as having an economic impact: the instability of family life, listlessness at school, a growing national tendency to corruption, or hedonism; an insensitivity to suffering; a callousness that breeds ugliness of behavior. I think that one such affliction is the failure to acknowledge a running debt to one's homeland (biological or adopted). That is one deficiency that national service seeks to accost. It will perhaps be argued that a psychic torpor can be noticed by the market. And, yes, such signals may be there, however amorphously rendered. The occasional analyst will refer to a "national mood," which however he quickly links to bearish stock exchanges. But such signals sound too faintly and too ambiguously to be heard save with the aid of a stethoscope at the hands of an active and intuitive intelli-

gence. Certainly such sounds as national anomie do
not sound imperatively enough to reconfigure a market
whose scanning mechanisms are insufficient to define
them, and which do not prescribe their own cure. The
call for more calamine is absolutely distinct. The call
for increased loyalty to the nation and its institutions
does not travel from the objective situation to the economist's computer screen.

It is illustrative to remark here the difference between hunger, say, and loneliness. Hunger, the primal
human instinct, demands satisfaction now. In exchange for sating the appetite, the hungry human
being will come up with tender satisfactory to the
farmer who provides the food. Loneliness is a condition not readily addressed by the market mechanism.
True, some who are lonely seek escapism—in drugs,
in sensation, in hectic distraction. They do not, experience reveals, find what they are looking for: the
search for the happy alcoholic begins and ends with
Harvey. The lonely human being is in search of one
or another form of love, of companionship. These are
not market commodities, issuing as they do from extra-
market sources. The patriotic spirit can be ostensibly
appeased by manufacturers of flags, and by bands that
play the works of John Philip Sousa. But the deep
wellsprings of patriotism are fed by other forces, and
these do not leave fingerprints in the market. They

must be investigated by the use of entirely different instruments.

The market operates, at least during the moment of the transaction, by satisfying both parties. The exchange of a pair of your shoes for a pair of my gloves leaves you better off than you were before, because you value the pair of gloves more than the redundant pair of shoes. It is manifest that some exchanges quickly sour: the happy investment in a Savings and Loan bond on Monday which on Tuesday becomes worthless.

The exchange, in such a system as would comprehend national service, isn't immediate and is not entirely predictable. Aunt Lucy derived a measure of satisfaction she would never have received, save for the service of her great-nephew Robert. And Robert found that he got satisfaction from ministering to the needs of Aunt Lucy, even as he took pleasure in ministering to others' needs. But this is the moment to underscore that in my judgment it is the benefits to Robert, even more than those to Aunt Lucy, that motivate my enthusiasm for national service. So much the better that she *feels* better, but there are forms of national service in which there is no specific Aunt Lucy in the picture. Work done designed to improve the environment is only dimly, remotely, and perhaps even ambiguously appreciated by those sensitive to environmental change. Work done to preserve from deterioration recondite books in the Library of Congress yields

satisfaction to the book mender, though he can't absolutely predict that the esoteric book whose preservation has occupied his day will in fact ever be
consulted in the next century by an aberrant scholar.
It is fine, splendid in fact, that national service can
anticipate solid good done to other human beings in
need, but that is not the governing justification of national service, in this assessment of its value. We look
primarily for something other.

Now it is very easy, and very tempting, to speak
primarily, even exclusively, about the good to be done
by national service participants. The argument for such
service rests on the proposition that there is surplus
human energy—i.e., energy not needed for subsis-
tence—that ought to be channeled to social needs
whose spokesmen cannot successfully plead their case
in the marketplace. Perhaps for that reason, skeptics
are afraid of an idea which they dismiss as one more
act of federal intervention, sought by social activists-
on-the-prowl, injustice collectors who look for opportunities to find needs that aren't acute enough to
generate economic demand, which needs can only
hope to attract the attention of affluent societies. But
these needs mirror, in the affluent society, a latent
appetite to serve those needs; an appetite to be sure,
in part sharpened because, on learning of someone's
loneliness, one would like to be instrumental in alle-
viating its pain; but in vital part because to do so is an

experience by which one obliges those sleeping angels
in one's own nature through which one develops the
best kind of pride.

Soon after his election, President George Bush
was asked just where and what were the "thousand
points of light." He was judged especially vulnerable
on the point by militant defenders of several programs
initiated by Presidents Johnson and Carter which
President Reagan, presumably with the sanction of his
vice president, had either diminished or, in one or two
cases, simply abolished. How could Mr. Bush speak
of points of light when he had been associated with
someone who went about dousing those lights?

To begin with, the critics of Mr. Bush assumed
that a point of light was the equivalent of a federal
program, an assumption quite simply unwarranted.
Beyond that, Mr. Bush was ably defended by James
Strock, Assistant Administrator for Enforcement in the
Environmental Protection Agency, in a spirited reply
to these critics. His rejoinder (parts of which were published in *Policy Review*) said that by the time he had
left the White House, Ronald Reagan had provided
the impulse and the means (the first by diminishing
inflation, interest rates, and unemployment; the second by a national inoculation of self-confidence that
dissipated the torpor associated with Mr. Carter's mal-
aise) to ignite many more than a thousand points of

light. He gave specific figures. Twenty-three million
people spent, in 1988, five hours per week or more in
volunteer social work of one kind or another—figures
collected by an organization called Independent Sector. Fifty-seven million give some of their time every
week, if less than five hours. This being so, over eighty
million Americans volunteer nearly a billion hours of
their time to activity generally thought of as philanthropic, or civic-minded: a contribution worth an estimated one hundred and fifty billion dollars. There is
no handy alternative to accepting the calculations of
Independent Sector, a Washington-based coalition of
700 corporations, foundations, and nonprofit organi-
zations whose purpose is to encourage philanthropy
and voluntary action. Their findings aren't counter-
intuitive. Do you spend five hours per week—a cumulative figure: remember, five hours can mean thirty
stretches of ten minutes—doing something for somebody else, this side of duties formally written into formal institutional arrangements? (I would not think of
a mother caring for her child or a husband helping to
wash the dishes as qualifying as a point of Mr. Bush's
light.) The figure is bracing. Eighty million people is
a very high percentage of the population (246 million),
so that if one excludes children (63.7 million under
age eighteen) and the very old (75+—12.5 million)
one is tempted to perceive the substantiality of something very far removed from a chimera: a huge body,

however inchoate, of unmet needs, finding its way to a huge appetite to meet their needs. This great, green pasture exists now outside the formal structures of the market and encourages the desire to augment the effort, in order further to satisfy the needy—but primarily in order to give scope to the impulses of those who desire to go to them. To help.

What are we talking about, concretely?

You receive a letter. It is from, oh, a prisoner. He tells you why he is really innocent. In order to plead his case, he most desperately needs—some encouragement, and, if possible . . . a typewriter. Perhaps you satisfy his first request, by writing to him in more than perfunctory detail, using up, say, a half hour of your time. Perhaps, even, you give him your old typewriter. A totally discrete transaction.

What else?

I think of a personal experience. Cardinal Hayes High School in New York City is located in the Bronx and is run by the Catholic Church. A few years ago that high school looked down on an accumulation of data that cried out for action. A fresh policy was born.

It transpired that the expense of teaching the incremental student at Cardinal Hayes was much lower than the cost per student per year in the public high schools. The second datum was that students educated by Cardinal Hayes did much better, judged by any

criterion, than students educated in the public high
schools. That is, a (far) greater percentage of the Hayes
students went on to matriculate in college; and, once
in college, a far higher percentage went on to complete
college.

But although the per-student costs are lower at
Cardinal Hayes, they are neither nonexistent nor in-
considerable, and the Catholic Archdiocese of New
York had long since resolved that the parochial schools
needed to raise the money they spent. In the year I
was introduced to the experiment, the per-student figure came to sixteen hundred dollars per student per
year for tuition. This figure contrasted with more than
$3,000 per student per year in a New York City public
high school. The challenge then became: How, without
a tax collector at one's side, do you raise sixteen
hundred dollars for a relatively indigent child?

The compassionate yet tough-minded administrators of the program imposed a further burden on
the program they would come to call the Student/
Sponsor Partnership. It was that no student for whom
help would be sought could come from a household
in which there were two resident parents. Let house-
holds in New York so blessed look after their children's
schooling as best they could: if they chose parochial
or other private schools, they would be expected to
come up with the money to pay their child's tuition.

So, ironies and realities: 1) No student from an

unbroken home. And then one more specification, 2) No student would be permitted to come in under the Student/Sponsor auspice who had shown extraordinary talent while at grammar school—i.e., no superhigh achiever. These students, once again, could make their way into the special schools, receive scholarships, and get on using their own resources. By the same token, at the other end of the scale, no student would be admitted whose record at grammar school was so low as to suggest that he (Cardinal Hayes takes only boys; there are complementary Catholic high schools, St. Michael's Academy and Cathedral High School, that take only girls) had slight prospects of graduating.

Enter the sponsor. The idea was to reach out and find sponsors who would do two things. First, come up with sixteen hundred dollars to back an individual student. Second, take a personal interest in the protégé, helping to motivate the student.

We have here an endeavor that already qualifies as national service: the adult sponsor gives cash to the school *and* takes the time to keep in touch with the student during the four years he spends at Cardinal Hayes. But there is more to it, much more.

The administrators of Cardinal Hayes needed to augment their staff with what one might call social tutors, young men who had finished college and could help to guide the sponsored student while at Cardinal Hayes by giving him practical help with his studies,

by encouraging him to work to meet the standards of
the school, by serving (I shrink from the term) as a Big
(non-Orwellian) Brother.

During two successive years I met two young men
who had volunteered to spend one year at Cardinal
Hayes before going on, in the first case to law school,
in the second to business school. These volunteers
worked for nominal wages, doing exactly the kind of
duties one would expect of a National Service volunteer. It was clear from even a brief encounter that they
were themselves highly motivated, intelligent, and
wholly aware of the meaning—of the value—of the
sacrifice they were making. That such activity already
goes on outside the framework of a formal national
service program shouldn't, given the gross figures cited
earlier, surprise us.

The point is that we are looking at an arrangement
that does not fit into the orthodox market schematic.
For one thing, the success of the Cardinal Hayes
Student/Sponsor program depends heavily on extra-
commercial mediation. *Someone* had to tell potential
sponsors about the existence of the Cardinal Hayes
program, describe its record of success; and then, by
suasion of sundry kinds, persuade them to become
sponsors.

One might reasonably suspect the powerful suasion is Catholicism itself. However, ninety-five percent
of the students entering Cardinal Hayes under the

Student/Sponsor program are black or Hispanic, and a majority are not Catholics. This is worth remarking, given the natural propensity to be attracted to the plight of one's own, even as, typically, white orphans are adopted by white parents, and liaisons sprout more readily among those of common ethnic background. The special plight of the black and Hispanic young people in New York City became a part of the objective challenge of altruistically inclined men and women associated with Cardinal Hayes. One cannot know how many potential white sponsors were put off by the racial composition of the program, but we must assume that some were, human nature being as human nature is. The salient fact remains that some—many—were not.

And then there are the young college graduate guides. I am not familiar with the means by which their cooperation was effected. Given that no sanctions that I know of were in place, the strength of their motivation must be regarded as unusual. Nor do we know how many young men simply listened to emissaries from Cardinal Hayes High School requesting that they donate a year of their time, and then walked away without signing up. What we can reasonably assume is that if sanctions were in place, sanctions of the kind we will speak of later, a much higher number of volunteers would enter the Cardinal Hayes program,

and others like it. And this is the more important datum, viewed from this perspective, than the augmen-
tation of the number of underprivileged children who
make it through high school and on to college: that
there should be an increase in volunteers and sponsors
who desire to help. The redemption of Scrooge was
more important, in *A Christmas Carol*, than the stuffed
goose or even Bob Cratchit's surprise.

That there are human needs untended by suppliers can be called an economic imperfection, but
ought not to be called that because the market
shouldn't be asked to perform functions for which it
is incompetent. Whether a society has altruistic reserves on which it will draw to help those who need
help is not a market question. And of course what
tends to separate the liberal from the conservative here
is the predisposition of the liberal to conscript the
whole of the community in order to help the afflicted
by the medium of taxation. Where dissent is focused,
the conservative tends to stress action by individual
states and, preferable to that, voluntary action by individuals.

National service doesn't lend itself to conventional
analysis. For this reason it pays to stress and re-stress
that the market has only a tangential role, if any, in
suggesting vectors of national service concern. The
idea, as viewed through the conservative looking glass,

is to arouse a desire which is uniquely one's own to help a society.

Inasmuch as we speak thus openly about the uses of the state to expedite a program designed to stimulate targeted human qualities, one needs instantly to face up to the charge that we are engaged in a grand manipulation of the human personality by the state. Our generation has observed the maximum enterprise of this kind, the victims of which were the Chinese people. Mao Tse-tung set out, no less, to create a New Man. Mao-man. He was to be the docile creature of the will of the state. The idea of Mao-man died, officially, at Tiananmen Square: died figuratively and literally. Tiananmen Square, followed so soon by the events in Eastern Europe, was the final, gratifying answer to George Orwell. If all the engines of Chinese Communism under Mao were insufficient to change human nature, it is unlikely that the resources of the state will ever be equal to that challenge. The state can rule, but it cannot command loyalty, let alone effect morphological changes in human nature.

It is feared by many opponents of national service that the use of state power in whatever form, even in a voluntary program, is nevertheless an effort, even if halfhearted, in that direction: an effort to change the human personality, and for that reason to be resisted categorically. In a spirited denunciation of the whole

idea of national service, done at a conference to examine the question at the Hoover Institution in September 1989, my friend and ideological colleague Dr.
Martin Anderson, using heated language, suggested
that national service is something like Guy Fawkes
inside a Trojan horse waiting to subvert American freedom. (Mr. Anderson began his paper by proclaiming
that ". . . one finds the sharp fangs of coercion and
compulsion, the faint whiff of envy and hatred of the
young, and the ideological yearning for elements of a
totalitarian society" in programs for national service.)
At the same conference Milton Friedman, my hero,
was quoted as finding in national service an "uncanny
resemblance" to the Hitler Youth Corps.

This last occasions only the reply that by that token, *all* youth programs, including the Boy Scouts, can
be likened, in the sense that they have *something* in
common, to the Hitler Youth program, plus the second
comment, that because Hitler had an idea, it does not
follow that that idea was bad. (Albert Speer is said to
have reflected, soon before his death, that it was a "pity
that Adolf Hitler disliked Picasso.")

As agreed, we should always be alert, confident
though the events of 1989 made us, to states which,
seeking to create thousand-year reichs, do so with
greater success than Romania, Czechoslovakia, Bul-
garia, Poland, and East Germany. But those nightmares seem remote. Some libertarians will never agree

with the Founding Fathers that a responsibility of the polity is to encourage virtue directly, through such disciplines as service in the militia, reverence for religious values, and jury service—the kind of thing Prime Minister Gladstone had in mind when he proposed "to establish a new franchise, which I should call—till a better phrase be discovered—the service franchise." Opponents of national service must establish, to make their case, that national service, unlike the state militia, or jury service, or military conscription in times of emergency, is distinctively hostile to a free society.

If national service can be perverted to inculcate docile submission to tyranny, one hears that it might also be the instrument of egalitarian levelers. Mr. Anderson actually insists that those who favor national service are furtively engaged in conscripting everyone to do the "dirty work" of society. "The basic thrust of their fringe philosophical view is that all the dirty, distasteful and dangerous work in any society *should be shared equally* [italics in the original] by all the people who live in the society. No exceptions, woman or man, rich or poor, skillful or not, every single soul must do his or her share of taking out the garbage, preparing the dead for burial, cleaning toilets, guarding violent prisoners, and taking care of those sick and dying from deadly, contagious diseases, for that is the moral imperative." I fear—while, of course, applauding his instinctive hostility to egalitarianism—that if Mr.

Anderson really chooses to press the moral offensive on this front, he is going to run into a biblical Gallipoli. I doubt that he really wants to do this, but he is certainly correct that national service cannot legitimately conceive of itself as an agent of the class struggle.

The founders of liberal society understood more clearly than some of their progeny the nature of the civic problem. Adam Smith admired Rome and the Greek republics in which "every free citizen was instructed, under the direction of the public magistrate, in gymnastic exercises and in music." These had as their purpose "to humanize the mind, to soften the temper, and to dispose it for performing all the social and moral duties both of public and private life." When Lincoln wondered whether government by the people of the people and for the people could long endure, he must surely have been asking himself whether a republic of freemen can regenerate itself—even as Hamilton had wondered about this, only a dozen years after Adam Smith had made his point. The concern of the Founding Fathers was variously expressed, during the time of Philadelphia and also later. The objective was to induce a virtuous citizenry. It was quite commonly accepted that this was likeliest to happen to the extent that religious principles governed human action. But it was also accepted, as witness the call by President Washington for universal military service, that a period of civic sacrifice heightened individual disposition to loyalty, to involvement in civil affairs, and to the identification of one's own interests with those of the community. The Civil War, of course, fragmented the larger idea of community loyalty, and the pieces have not completely come back together, save when a Pearl Harbor, or a two hundredth anniversary celebration comes around. And then there was generated, partly as a reaction against the birth of the great totalitarian societies, a suspicion of any role by the state in ventures of the sort we are here to describe. The instinctive suspicions of such as Professor Martin Anderson are probably healthy. But they should yield to calm analysis. Much of what we observe going on in the United States, particularly among youth, so distinguished an observer clearly cannot be tranquil about. And so one appeals from Philip drunk to Philip sober to sit down, think . . . and have another look at national service.

☆   ☆   ☆   ☆   ☆   ☆   ☆   ☆   ☆   ☆   ☆

The Citizen's Obligations; The Citizen's Needs

*T*he conviction of some conservatives that the state can't have a genuine, non-predatory interest in the cultivation of virtue strikes me as an anarchical accretion in modern conservative thought, something that grew from too humorless a reading of such spirited individualists as Albert Jay Nock and H. L. Mencken. A useful way to approach the question is by the *reductio ad absurdum*. In *The Federalist Papers*, Hamilton wrote bluntly that the republic had no prospect of survival in the event of a general distemper of the people, and this would appear to be obvious. It is easy to imagine (and frightening to do so) the result of a refusal by the minority to abide by the licit authority of the majority. What then happens goes by the pejorative of banana republicanism.* And yet it takes conditioning to abide by democratic practice. It is not a genetically inherited practice, as we can see by surveying the relative scarcity of functioning democracies in the world in modern times. It requires training of sorts, and the state incorporates the will of the people in prescribing the laws that, for instance, give power to one political party as distinguished from another.

Manifestly, republican government has an interest in inculcating in its citizens the obligations of the political minority (as well as the obligations of the political majority).

On the other hand, it is obvious that there is much to fear from the enhancement and enlargement of the state. James Madison was correct when he averred that the state uses "the old trick of turning every contingency into a resource for accumulating force in the government." National service, if transformed merely into a state bureaucracy with huge powers of intimi-

* I remember one afternoon, in the editorial offices of *National Review*, when the Associated Press nonchalantly reported that the Republic of Bolivia had just lost its government to a military rebellion, the 192nd overthrowing of leadership since its inception, an editor proposed, as a fitting proclamation for the new government, the start of official preparations for a major national celebration upon achieving the two hundredth Bolivian coup d'état.

dation, is not only to be avoided, it is to be fought. But we can open our minds to something other than a statist program, or one that lodges in the state the kind of power conservatives have been taught, at great historical expense, to husband for social uses. The state needs at once to be used, to "work," and to be kept at bay; and the eternal question, of course, is, How to bind the citizen to the state without being bound by it?

In the Middle Ages, the search was for intermediate institutions, institutions that would stand between the subject and the sovereign. There was, supremely, the Church. And then came the guilds. The latter were anachronized by the Industrial Revolution, but in their absence the effort continues to conjure up the idea of communitarian fraternity, and to seek out forms in which the idea of community might be usefully embodied.

Now, "fraternity" is here a word one needs to pause over, inasmuch as the French Revolution, in enshrining that word, in effect committed parricide. The French revolutionists may have been brothers, but now they had no fathers. The symbol of French fatherhood was guillotined in broad daylight amidst a delighted frenzy. And with the king's head went any formal sense of obligation to the past; to the patrimony. Jacobin constitutional doctrine was to be exnihilated, created from nothing, following the example of Rousseau, who had sat down to write an ideal constitution for the government of Poland as if any thought given to Polish culture were somehow irrelevant. For all its communitarian slogans, the French Revolution represented, as Burke clearly saw, a kind of amputation from the past, genocide against French cultural ancestry. That the French Revolution never really came off is the reason why we can talk about French civilization with a straight face.

And then of course Marxist thought crystallized. Under Marxism, the patrimony is simply a historical epoch, or stage, in the continuing historical dialectic that would one day yield a condition of utopian statelessness. The incumbent class was the class produced by a collision with and absorption of the predecessor class, which would itself, in conflict with its looming antithesis, produce the succeeding class, and so on. This idea became deep-frozen with the advent of the Soviet nomenklatura and its satraps, getting not very far, though creating great suffering for tens of millions.

Meanwhile the Catholics, animated mostly by Leo XIII and his famous encyclical Rerum Novarum (1891), set out in search of social bonds, reacting against the mechanistic liberalism that was thought to have overwhelmed other, more important values and loyalties. The idea was that a kind of "corporatism" was the way to go; and for several decades, in Europe and Latin America, corporatism was popular not only

among Catholics but among secularists who sought an
alternative to the liberalism of the Industrial Revolution and the social Darwinism associated with it. For
the working man, the labor union was to be the principal unit of social cohesion, after the family. The state
would have the bureaucracy, and, together with the
union, would work in harmony, creating something on
the order of the syndicalism that later excited the
proto-fascists.

This was variously experimented with, uniformly
without success. The unions became primarily instruments of economic pressure—nothing much more
than their own expression of that mechanistic liberalism against which the Pope had warned. And, of
course, the cooptation of the unions by the bureaucracy
forwarded fascism of various kinds, including the militant and ideological fascism of Mussolini's Italy in
which the state became precisely that object so correctly feared by genuine republicans: the central unit
of undifferentiated loyalty.

There were exceptions, of course. There were, and
there are, labor unions that serve fraternal purposes
even as there are bureaucratic units that sometimes
seem more like surviving guilds than like instruments
of the state. But this is to compare the twenty-fifth
reunion of a fighting battalion with a fighting battalion.
Nothing really emerged in the way of a viable, growing
institutional body that claimed the correct kind of loy-

alty of the citizen and that cultivated in the citizen something on the order of virtue: hardly a competitor to the church, on which the obligation primarily falls to cultivate a knowledge of virtue and a taste for it; nothing that could remind the citizen that there is more to his relationship to his country than the willingness to fight for its survival by dying for it if necessary, and the workaday commitment to pay taxes to maintain its overhead.

But the search for an experience that helps to anneal the citizen's bond to his country is indisputably an ongoing search, and its success should be thought of as indisputably enhancing the prospects of a happy and useful understanding of the reason why free men should be grateful: among such reasons, that they know a form of gratitude is required in order to enhance the prospects of remaining free.

On obligations: It is realistic to conclude that a national service program entirely voluntary in nature, i.e., a program lacking in persuasive inducements, is likely to founder. There is no reason to be surprised by this, given that most of what human beings do is in response to sanctions or inducements of one kind or another: God, self, family, health, patriotism. Organized inducements are appropriate and are not in conflict with a conservative understanding of the relationship between the state and the citizen, whose

education is to a certain stage properly required; whose
services in the military are, in extremis, conscriptable;
whose taxes are reasonably exacted. That the people
themselves should take an interest in the development
of the ethos appropriate to republican freemen ought
not to surprise. We are, after all, self-governing, and
our interest in what we wish to sustain is in two parts.
Most frequently, we vote—to head in this or the other
direction, with this or the other proposed public policy,
under this, or that, leader. Another stage concerns itself with the prescriptive guidelines by which we are
governed, our ideas of what is right, what wrong; and
our derivative concern with a society that seems not to
be effectively transmitting, to our successor citizens,
those ideas we cling to as indispensable to the char-
acterization of a proud society. It is not a distortion of
its responsibilities when the state, sensing dissatisfaction, or anxiety, lends its mechanisms to the transcrip-
tion of the nature of that popular dissatisfaction. To
do so, it asks that we examine our misgivings, and, if
we feel that the shared experience of national service
is desirable or even necessary, that we instruct the state
to cooperate in an effort to institutionalize it. Cooperate
by exploring the range of tolerable and persuasive inducements, negative and positive, to get it started.

Clearly it matters that there should be avenues for
the expression of the altruistic impulse. These avenues
have become common in the welfare state. The public

is uneasy about malnourishment, or hunger? A lobby arises, presents itself as expressing public concern, a majority is mobilized behind it, and then a legislative act is consummated, and soon little green—brown— blue stamps issue. National service, on the other hand, poses unorthodox problems of democratic action. The impulse is there (we know from the public polls and from intuition and experience), but resistance is (happily) considerable to making it one more arm of the welfare state.

How then to communicate to our legislators what it is that is wanted, while communicating at the same time what it is that is most definitely not wanted? We need to devise the means of exposing the public to a program that will gratify its desires while dispelling its doubts. Many citizens, though restless with the seeming absence of vehicles that might absorb their civic sense of obligation, or altruism, are benumbed by thoughtlessness. If alerted to the possibility of making a positive gesture of gratitude to the patrimony, something not overfreighted with taxation or compulsion, they are, in my judgment, most likely to react enthusiastically. Some others with less than enthusiasm, but they are the challenge—to awaken in them the sense of civic pride that our schoolteachers are charged with awakening in our children, and to suggest real forms by which the pursuit of that civic pride might take on special, creative meaning. To do this requires the use of inducements, and of sanctions. A reliance on "discriminatory" acts—hateful word, given the ugliness of the discrimination historically practiced by racists; but even as fraternity needs to be rescued from the Jacobins, discrimination needs to be rescued from Jim Crow.

Before we speak of inducements, we need of course to confront the primary question of the right of organized society to impose discriminations with the view to achieving its ends. How are constitutionally well-mannered Americans, brought up in the tradition of freedom and equality, going to be persuaded to press their case for institutionalizing a newfound sense of obligation?

☆　☆　☆　☆　☆　☆　☆　☆　☆　☆　☆

Two Classes of Citizens

*L*iberals are more attracted to organized welfare, centrally managed, than conservatives. Moreover, they tend to balk less at regimentation, unless it is military conscription for unpopular military actions.

We have in the question of compulsory national service extra-market factors pressing on a concrete situation seeking to affect human behavior. Free market reductionists will argue that the volunteer is putting a price on his own satisfaction, and that the satisfaction he feels in having given a year of his life to, say, the students of Cardinal Hayes becomes a palpable market force—i.e., he has paid a price and received rewards in return. (It is reasoning of this order that led Ayn Rand to deplore, and even to deny the meaning of, altruism.) Those who believe that national service *ought to be* desired by the majority are engaged in encouraging inclinations in young and old that are altruistic and civic-minded in nature; and some of us are prepared to prod them into active life by the use of positive and negative sanctions.

The introduction of sanctions, of rewards and denials, suggesting a division between those on whom pressure needs to be applied and those on whom the sense of responsibility comes naturally, puts us in the way of consolidated liberal (and, indeed, conservative) doctrine to the effect that there must not be different classes of citizens. This is a generality with roots at different levels of social and theological thought. Those who believe that all men are equal in the eyes of God make a primary commitment to equality of one kind, which however does not necessarily correspond either to social or to political equality, or, for that matter, theological equality (it can be argued by orthodox theologians that God prefers the saint to the sinner, always provided it is understood that overnight the sinner can, and in the historical past often has, become a saint. Augustine is the locus classicus). When the Declaration of Independence declared that all men are created equal it spoke affirmatively about natural rights, not about social status, income, or even civil liberties.

But along the way attention ceased to attach to distinctions once commonplace. At the same time our neglect of other distinctions has made it difficult, in a republic, to speak about broad questions of status among citizens. These distinctions can be traced most directly to Aristotle and to Thomas Aquinas, and there is no need to reiterate them here at any length. It is enough to say that it is a solid part of our social history to acknowledge different forms of justice that inhere, without difficulty, under the tent of equality.

Thomas speaks of "general justice," which takes the good of the whole community as its object and would, for instance, be invoked to justify the quarantine of diseased persons. After that comes particular justice, and this is of two orders, the one "commutative," the other, "distributive." These distinctions survive whole in the Lockean tradition, even if they are not so designated. The Founding Fathers never denied the primacy of such matters as the survival of the state (indeed it was their concern with it that caused them to move from the Articles of Confederation to the Constitution). And Jefferson's affirmation of the rights of everyone to life, liberty, and the pursuit of happiness was never thought to exclude differences in achievement or in rank.

In respect of the duty of the government to promote good behavior, there was, again, no doubt. Acknowledging his First Inaugural Address, the Senate addressed a reply to George Washington (May 18, 1789): "We feel, Sir, the force and acknowledge the justness of the observation, that the foundation of our national policy should be laid in private morality. If individuals be not influenced by moral principles, it is in vain to look for public virtue; it is, therefore, the duty of legislators to enforce, both by precept and example, the utility as well as the necessity, of a strict adherence to the rules of distributive justice."

Commutative justice treats people without distinction. (The law of contract is the same for the plumber and for the President.) But this is not so in distributive justice, to which idea one appeals in considering sanctions of the kind that would separate those willing from those not willing to undertake special civic duties. It is important, in order to feel one's way about the subject, to bear in mind that distributive justice acknowledges differences in individual orders. These distinctions (in the medieval view) are conferred primarily by act of a central moral authority—the father, the regime—which is not necessarily guided by the meritocratic imperative. If you were the firstborn of the local duke, your privileges, compared with those of your brother, extended out of sight; and this fruit of distributive justice was not challenged. But then neither was it challenged when you and not your brother were made wealthy by a fortunate marriage arranged by your godfather. Thomas Gilby, a Thomist

scholar, has summarized the point: "Distributive justice . . . was not egalitarian but aristocratic, for it
bestowed wealth, honors, and jobs in alterable proportions whether that was measured by initiative, own-
ership, or excellence of character. *Justice here meant
dealing unequally with unequal men.*"

The citizen who feels the impulse to repay his debt
to society by volunteering his service, and does, is to
be distinguished from the citizen who does not. The
first has primary claims to the society's good graces.
But it is of critical importance that the opportunity to
qualify be universal.

Conservatives need, I think, to be reminded of this
order of justice. They accept it readily enough where
the military veterans are concerned—they are entitled
to their G.I. Bill of Rights and to special care at the
veterans' hospital. The task is to move the imagination
across the mental, mechanical barrier, the barbed wire
within which it has for so many generations been
sealed. The distinguished sociologist Robert Nisbet acknowledges the claims of community, and that these
are claims even when they are not summonses. The
citizen who neglects his children is truly and significantly different from the citizen who does not, irre-
spective of the law (where there is one) that classifies
the first as guilty of a misdemeanor, the second as not
guilty. An accumulation of these distinctions is em-

bodied in the idea of national service, and this is an
early plea that the conservative should shake loose
from his disposition to reject out of hand as a statist
presumption any gesture in the direction of acknowledging different orders of citizenship. That line of de-
marcation should exist, among other reasons, in order
to prompt those on the nether side to traverse it. It is
frequently said of America that it is hard to find many
persons living here who think of themselves as members of the lower class. So would one hope that, sometime in the future, it will be hard to find anyone who
confessed, in respect of failing to repay his country's
legacy with a year's service, to living on the freeloaders'
side of the tracks.

The liberal is usually quick to insist that the market does not by any means perform a moral duty—that
any number of social needs go unremarked by its ru-
dimentary, indeed crass mechanisms. Yet he is likely
to balk at the notion that an appropriate corrective, as
here suggested, is one whose implementation would
leave us with citizenship of different orders. The
liberal-egalitarian will object to the divisive character
of such distinctions, his efforts having, over the years,
gone toward eliminating distinctions, not to pointing
them up. Not long ago, in pursuit of this dream, the
republic was persuaded to abandon election laws that
required of the aspirant voter that he prove he could

read and write. In theory, the liberal is likely to object, national service of the kind toward which this essay points is an invitation to social polarization.

But in order even to talk about sanctions, plus and minus, we need to confront a hardy preconception, which is that there is only the single category of American citizens. No one will wish to repeal the right of all Americans to the equal protection of the laws. This is a birthright one forfeits only by committing felonies. But to acknowledge the common birthright of all citizens is not to acknowledge identical rights for all citizens, at all levels.

Only quite recently was it proposed that because a citizen has the right to the protection of the laws, it follows that he also has the right to participate in the definition of these laws. To do that—to vote—he once had to know how to read and write. Earlier in our history, in an age properly stigmatized for such discrimination, to vote one had to be a male; and before that, one had to be a white male and, concurrently, one had to own property in the district in which one aspired to vote. And if one owned property in more than one district, one could vote twice, as so many Englishmen did in the early years of the nineteenth century.

These are preferential distinctions that are in my judgment indefensible, and in any event aren't going to be defended here. But to say as much is not to say that distinctions of any kind are indefensible. In a country where we would take the obligation of national service to heart (where it belongs, as well as in the mind), a public acknowledgment of the difference between the two classes—those who have participated in national service, and those who have not—would be in order, whatever forms of distinction the people, acting through their legislatures, proceed to select as appropriate. There's no point in denying that we are looking, prospectively, at what would amount to, in the public eye, first- and second-class citizens: those who do, over against those who do not, attempt to requite their debt to their country.

The concept of a "first-class citizen" and a "second-class citizen" could crystallize in the public mind without disturbing the universal commitment to equal birthrights, or our zeal to guard the machinery of upward mobility. Even so, sometime in the future, perhaps thirty or forty years from now, those capable of doing so who had not performed national service would be thought of as second-class citizens. If taxation, for example, were voluntary, one would reasonably distinguish, where income was comparable, between those who paid their taxes, helping to defray the cost of schools, firemen, policemen, soldiers, sanitation workers, and other public services, and those who did not: the freeloaders, the shirkers. Though taxes are involuntary, national service should not be.

It does not for that reason follow that those who fail to do their duty should go unnoticed.

You can see the problems you get into when both acknowledging and trying to avoid the implications of first- and second-class citizenship by tracking the evolution of the thought of Professor Charles C. Moskos, who is the principal architect of the Nunn bill, the most prominent national service bill introduced in 1989. He is the author of the book *A Call to Civic Service*, deservedly prominent in the literature of national service.

It is instructive to weigh Mr. Moskos's arguments, as well as amusing to do so. He is courageous enough to recount his own harried odyssey on the subject of national service. What happens (in his book) is:

1) He begins by listing as the most serious objection to a national service proposal only the suggestion that it should be other than compulsory. "Unless national service is universal, it would aggravate already existing divisions in American society."

2) He goes on to quote an eloquent defense of the compulsory position: "A voluntary national service program would probably evolve into a two-track system; a lower one trying to 'salvage' poverty-scarred youth, and a higher one offering upper-middle-class youth a channel to resolve identity crises through altruistic endeavors. Those national service programs that would appeal to upper-middle-class college youth on a voluntary basis could easily turn into new forms

of institutional elitism. At the same time, national service programs directed toward lower-class youth would
be quickly defined for what they are—welfare schemes
in new guises. Any effective national service program
will necessarily require coercion to insure that all seg-
ments of the American class structure will serve."

3) Whereupon he reveals that the author of those
stentorian lines supporting compulsory service was—
Professor Moskos, in the bad-old-days when he took
the position that national service should be compulsory.

4) I say bad-old-days because he now writes that
national service needs to be voluntary. Professor Martin Anderson has challenged the sincerity of Professor
Moskos's change of heart, at the Hoover Institution
seminar mentioned earlier.

"Over the years, Moskos's lust for compulsion
never dimmed. 'If I could have a magic wand, I would
be for a compulsory system,' Moskos told *Time* magazine when asked about national service in 1987. Then
he bragged to a columnist for the *Chicago Tribune* that
his latest effort, the legislation introduced by Senator
Sam Nunn of Georgia in 1989, was 'just this side of
compulsion, but we don't cross the line.' "

What caused Moskos finally to renounce a compulsory national service, he tells us, is his "linchpin
proposal to give priority, and eventually sole eligibility,
for post-secondary school benefits to national servers,

a qualitative leap from any other volunteer scheme. My fear at the time I wrote the words quoted above— that the prevailing youth philosophy would only reinforce the existing split between elite Peace Corps/ VISTA participants and poor Job Corps enrollees— anticipated what actually came to pass in the 1970s."

Professor Moskos discreetly conditions the shock, and indeed succeeds in drawing attention away from the implications of his proposal. He begins by briefly characterizing what he identifies as the two banners under which most of young America have marched in the post-Kennedy years. It began with President Kennedy's inaugural saying, "Ask not what your country can do for you; ask what you can do for your country." This injunction, he correctly observes, was very quickly inverted: for a while it seemed that almost everyone, everywhere, was asking, in effect, What *more* might the country do for them? (not least, shield them from exposure to North Vietnamese firepower).

The Kennedy period, Mr. Moskos informs us, was followed by the leave-me-alone-and-screw-the-national-interest debauch he associates with the Reagan Administration.

But now, Moskos believes, we are ready to march together under a synergistic banner enjoining us to do everything we can for our country, while our country does everything it can for us.

Yet his own linchpin plan draws a line between

the privileged and the less privileged, even as the G.I.
Bill did—those too young to be drafted and too poor
to pay their own way did not go to college, to which
all veterans had financial access. Professor Moskos
correctly attaches importance to what amounts to a
National Service Bill of Special Rights. But let's face
it, in so proposing he is acknowledging a measurement
of the kind of inequality that so appalled him in 1971.

Let it be. A society that strives after the enhancement of the commonly recognized virtues must encourage, not discourage, civic distinctions, always
provided there is perpetual mobility across the tracks.
The example set by the more virtuous citizen is a force
for the good. To suggest that it is divisive is on the
order of frowning on Eagle Scouts because their mere
existence discourages the mass of Tenderfoots.

It would be a welcome development if the whole
of a society embraced the common virtues. They do
not, and we save time by acknowledging that the whole
of society will never listen to the better angels within
our nature, any more than any individual will always
do so. It is a waste of time to evaluate a program on
the basis of its likelihood to effect 100 percent com-
pliance. The measure of the success of national service
is the extent to which it becomes truly national and
the extent to which, through example and the use of
inducements and sanctions, American youth are en-
couraged to give expression in some concrete way to

their gratitude for liberties inherited and protected. The introduction of sanctions is important because it increases the probable number of participants in national service to the point of isolating not those who serve, as is the case today (in the Peace Corps, e.g.), but those who do not serve. If two students in a class of forty decline to cheat, they run the risk of being objects of condescending derision. If thirty students decline to cheat, the others become not the arbiters of moral conduct, but refugees from norms that govern a majority clearly more high-minded.

☆　☆　☆　☆　☆　☆　☆　☆　☆　☆　☆

Chimeras: Wars on Poverty, Etc.

"Every year," Mr. Moskos informs us in his book on national service, "some 70,000 books in the Library of Congress crumble between their covers. At least 40 percent of the books in major research collections in the United States will soon be too fragile to handle. Preservation or microfilming of this collection is tedious and extremely labor intensive. We are [risking the loss of] a large portion of our cultural and intellectual heritage."

From all of the above we can conclude several things. The first is that, in the situation described, as in so many others, positive and weighable good will come to beneficiaries of national service. The second is that whatever the benefits to the recipients of such service, national service is not, and ought not to be conceived as, a welfare program. While acknowledging the good that can be done to the various beneficiaries, we reiterate that we have primarily in mind the good that is done to the volunteers themselves. There is, for instance, no need for confusion when reflecting on the national service volunteer who spends one year at the Library of Congress preserving a few thousand volumes from rot. Consider the young woman who takes on the library assignment. Perhaps she has the imagination to envision those who, in future years, will be able to read the books she has tended; perhaps she has not. But she will have experienced something, however impalpably: the tie to her civilization, and also the tie to her country. The former she is helping to sustain by preserving the literary corpus that is the achievement of civilization and indeed the documents by which that civilization guides itself. In respect of the *patria*, she is engaged in making a contribution—to the longevity of books over which someone once labored, and from which someone has received in the past, and may again in the future, pleasure and instruction. When the beneficiary is a victim of Alzheimer's disease, the volunteer experiences a direct tie to the life cycle and, as with our Robert Ely who spent one year with the Owlwood Retirement

Home, his perspective is altered. He has come to realize that he too was helped when as an infant he was helpless, and that the day may come when, toward the end of his life, he will be helpless again, and will reach out for help. And just as he has helped to sustain the faith of those currently afflicted, so is he buoyed by the knowledge that there was dormant in him the impulse to help to sustain their faith. This impulse slowly shaped up in his mind as an act of gratitude.

Whatever one's reservations about the benefits to the national service participant, there is one decisive way to sentence national service to death, and that is to conceive of it as a fight against poverty. The diminution of poverty is properly a national objective, but to confuse it with national service is to play the sorcerer's apprentice: Only confusion and chaos will result from tampering with the suitable formula. Writing in *The New Republic* in the fall of 1988, staffer James Bennet shredded candidate George Bush's espousal of the program "Youth Engaged in Service to America" (YES). It is a program which, for reasons other than those cited by Mr. Bennet, is in fact pretty jejune. But here is how Mr. Bennet put it:

"Pure voluntarism [in national service], as espoused by the Reagan-Bush administration, asks the private sector to fill gaps created by American capitalism and vacated by a retreating federal government; essentially, it leaves the war on poverty in the hands of vigilantes."

What's wrong with that statement, to begin with, is that capitalism doesn't "create" poor people. It incidentally identifies poor people by contrasting them with non-poor people, who are the most eloquent beneficiaries of capitalism. At this writing, the official division in America is 13 percent poor, 87 percent non-poor, which is relatively, if not absolutely, necessary, considering that at the turn of the century, using constant dollars and current criteria on where to draw the poverty line, 90 percent of Americans were poor. Moreover, voluntarism isn't vigilantism, a sinister social impulse; it is a sign of moral life that does no harm to our economic life. Between 1983 and the time of Mr. Bush's speech at least sixteen new programs of the kind that would qualify as national service activity were begun in twelve states of the union, none of them dependent on the federal government for one penny.

Indeed, the implicit position of Mr. Bennet, as of so many others, is that a social program is not serious unless funded by the federal government: ". . . as Bush confesses in promising to spend lots of money on 'YES,' the points of light don't shine quite so brightly when they're not plugged in to the federal treasury. This admission—that the government must play an

assertive role in helping the have-nots—places Bush
on traditionally Democratic turf. His dramatic un-
veiling of 'YES' to America demonstrates that he
doesn't know the territory.''

What brought all of this on was the specific en-
dorsement by President-elect Bush, as mentioned, of
the YES program which was estimated to cost (a mere)
$100 million. Yes, one hundred million federal dollars;
but such sums are deemed trivial by big social thinkers.
Their assumption is that any proposal is emasculated
that doesn't call for federal funding on a very large
scale. Such critics are seldom given to examining funds
already being spent to advance goals manifestly un-
attained. Mr. Bennet is undeterred by the trillion dollars spent by federal agencies since the federal poverty
programs were launched under Lyndon Johnson—
which programs, as Charles Murray has documented
in *Losing Ground*, are in most fearful disarray, with
shifting and sometimes shiftless patterns of unemployment, drug consumption, illegitimacy, crime,
homelessness, and illiteracy rising faster than poverty
is declining.

What the Bennet school of criticism wishes to see
in national service is a full-scale war against poverty.
"According to the YES position paper, Bush believes
'that the most important principle is the time given,
even five hours a week.' " Time given, i.e., by volun-

teers. "Wrong. The most important principle is the
effect on poverty of the time given." Again: federal
programs, munificently funded.

Consider the question of illiteracy, more closely
tied to the incidence of poverty than any other factor.
The statistics in general circulation tell us that 13
percent of Americans are functionally illiterate. We
are talking, then, about twenty-five million people,
more or less. Now any "program" that accosts the
problem of illiteracy macrocosmically—that is to say,
accosts it as one might a plague—cannot hope to deal
with it economically, let alone by the use, primarily,
of volunteers, however useful volunteer work among
illiterates demonstrably is. We are up against the difference between healing a child you spot suffering
from malnutrition and setting out to abolish malnutrition. To argue the desirability and the partial efficacy
of the first option is not to argue against accepting
simultaneously the strategic challenge (to abolish illiteracy). But you cannot accomplish the elimination
of twenty-five million Xs by so simple an arrangement
as multiplying by twenty-five million the adventitious
elimination of a single X, effected in spontaneous circumstances. This essay is not about abolishing illiteracy. It is animated first by the effect on the individual
volunteer who in his year's service succeeds in leading
a half dozen Americans up from illiteracy, and sec-

ondarily by the diminution, thereby, of the total number of illiterates. This is not to gainsay a national
program that seeks to do something about the curious
coexistence of compulsory schooling and an awesome
rate of illiteracy.

It is the confusion between federally financed,
macrocosmically conceived projects, and otherwise-
financed, volunteer-supported spot programs that re-
sults in unclear thinking on the subject of national
service. Different lobbies for national service have different objectives in mind. Moreover, the temptation is
not always resisted to doubt the seriousness of the cre-
dentials of spokesmen of the other school. Thus, for
instance, a scorching renunciation of George Bush's
YES program published, again, in *The New Republic.*
It charges that the entire pattern of President Reagan's
responses to social-philanthropic enterprise has been
one of "not-so-benign neglect." It goes on to cite a bill
of particulars. The Reagan Administration "killed"
Young Volunteers in Action and "contracted the budget" for Student Community Service Project and for
the office of Project Demonstration and Development.
How dare his successor, under the circumstances,
speak of his vision of a thousand points of light?

And then, to compound the record of neglect and
triviality, Mr. Bush comes to town and lays out his own
budget—a scanty $100 million to activate his entire
youth service program! By contrast, the bill introduced

by Senator Nunn, while not specifying a dollar figure in the introductory fanfare, was discreetly advertised as envisioning an expense of $7 billion. (By the way, an estimate so modest, given the bill's scope, that even in the early days of discussion it was not taken seriously by anyone who had given any attention to the historical costs of comprehensively ambitious programs.)

This commentary is fair up to a point. It is correct that neither Mr. Reagan nor Mr. Bush has given fruitful thought to a national service plan, and one result of this is that there have been scattered reactions, some routine, some studious, to individual programs. And it is undoubtedly true that many advocates of national service are enticed by the thought of directing a few million eighteen-year-olds, whose labor is inexpensive, to tidy up the dusty corners of the Welfare State.

But once again we are reminded of the difficulty so many of the millenarians suffer from, which is the eternal ambition to eliminate Skid Row. It is regularly left to crabby conservatives to point out that poverty will almost always be defined as that condition in which, roughly, the lowest-earning quintile of Americans live, never mind reassuring historical comparisons between the material level of life led by the poor of 1990, and the level of life in which families judged relatively affluent by contemporary evaluation lived earlier in the century.

When we are told that the poor are the primary

beneficiaries of national service—whether in their capacity as eighteen-year-old volunteers, or as indigent
aged in need of menial help—all we are being told is
that the poor need more help than the non-poor. Michael Kinsley, as editor of *The New Republic*, fore-
shadowed the Bennet thesis in a syndicated column in
which he weighed national service proposals on scales
that measured only benefits projected for poor vs. non-
poor. Anticipating the shape of the Nunn-Moskos bill,
he chose to criticize it primarily because he anticipated
that, faced with national service, middle-class young
would opt for military service and, in so doing, edge
out the poor who, nowadays, tend to subscribe heavily
to the volunteer military. If more affluent Americans,
in order to fulfill their obligations to national service,
end up by doing a stint in the military, that means that
many places less for the poor who wish to do *their*
service in the military and in any case are attracted to
the military by the relatively high pay the voluntary
military pays in order to attract the requisite soldiery.

He is making two points. The first that military
service pays a premium for enlistment—because life
is hard in the military, and contingently dangerous;
and second, that therefore military service, as a
form of service acceptable in discharge of general obligations to national service, would be ill-advised inasmuch as it is a vehicle especially suited to the
advancement of the poor. He is right, in my judgment,

that military service shouldn't count as national service, though I give different reasons for arguing the point (see below). And on the question of the distinctive danger associated with the military, one can only reflect that there is danger also in a career as a fireman or a policeman or a bodyguard. These dangers are compensated for in myriad ways, nicely worked out by the marketplace by suppliers and buyers. A one- or two-year stint in the military ought not, as I say, to exempt the soldier from national service duty.

Mr. Kinsley's objections might have earned more extensive confutation if one could reasonably look forward in the years ahead to a military of the 2–3 million size. Recent events in Eastern Europe and the Soviet Union suggest that this is unlikely. It is one thing to keep up one's guard, preserving the flexibility needed for contingent arrangements; something else to project what no longer seems likely, namely the need for a very large military. Its diminution causes us to focus, as already suggested, on civic alternatives as the vehicle for the exercise in citizenship which is, or ought to be, a national concern.

Although our emphasis is properly on the effects of national service on its participants, there should never be any temptation to adopt the Keynesian makework model in economics (Lord Keynes, in stressing the need for using unemployed labor, opined that in the absence of productive things to do, pyramid-building would be an acceptable activity). If the Keynesian temptation is altogether to be avoided, it will be so because there are now, and will be as far forward as we can see, genuine alternatives that make cynical approaches to work unnecessary. These alternatives, these needs, cannot be denied by anyone reflecting on the America we live in.

☆ ☆ ☆ ☆ ☆ ☆ ☆ ☆ ☆ ☆ ☆

The Range of Activity

*W*hen I was a boy and was sent off to boarding school at age fifteen I found myself under the direction of a man of great self-assurance who ran the school he had founded without any demoralizing doubts to the effect that others might run it better. It was *his* school, and the feature of its life that comes here to mind he called "Community Service." Several hours of every week, it was ordained, would be given to community service, and boys were authorized to select from among the dozen or more alternative ways to provide such service. If your interest was in naturalism, or in animals, you could clean the zoo, stuff birds, classify

fauna—the naturalist's options were seemingly endless. Or you could turn to agriculture, studying the
cultivation of flowers and vegetables, and creating a
garden. There was general housework to be done,
clearing the skating rink of snow, helping with routine
maintenance. I was placed in charge of the student
bank—every student had a checkbook made out on
that bank and it was my job, never mind that I'd rather
have been doing something else, to cash those checks
during "banking hours," and to balance the account
of the Strong Box, as it was called.

The war came, and duties proliferated. An alarm-
ist tied in to civil defense announced his fear that Nazi
warplanes would one day cross the Atlantic Ocean on
a bombing run, presumably to interior America. Our
school was located, on any reasonable trajectory from
Europe, beyond Boston, and before New York. It occurred to me only very much later that Lloyds of London would probably have given odds of a million to
one that no Nazi warplane would venture over Dutchess County, even in the black winter of 1942–43. But
the school took most seriously the call for volunteers
to take watches between dark and sunrise, looking for
the distinctive profiles of Nazi airplanes. In order to
qualify as a plane-watcher, one needed, of course, to
take a Community Service course in plane identification, a course taught by a teacher I had for years
found studiously, provocatively officious, who did not

in me, at least—although he did in others—stimulate the juices of learning. In any event I had a terrible time, staring at forty models of different Nazi fighters and bombers, in trying to distinguish one from another, which I would of course need to do if, staring at the sky one midnight, I should see one soaring over me. My fear was that I would lurch to the telephone and call in to the designated Army Air Force field the wrong plane. The penalty for not passing my plane-spotting test would be the suspension of my most treasured privilege, which was leave to take my little light-weight motorbicycle (manufactured in Germany, and purchased the preceding summer in Mexico with money borrowed from my father) and putt-putt the twelve cold miles to my home, to relax for a day and a half in the company of my parents, or siblings, or whoever happened to be in residence on weekends. The threat drove me to frenzies of effort. During that exertion one of my sisters, who was working in New York for United Press, relayed the unforgettable story of an event in the preceding week. Somewhere in England, a housewife had been honored for having correctly identified the new German light bomber, a Messerschmitt 210 or whatever, which the RAF were desperate to bring down for purposes of exploration. She had called in her information, the RAF had quickly dispatched a fighter squadron, the German plane was downed, and an army of technicians de-

scended on it to unearth whatever was new in Nazi
aeronautical technology. In recognition of her services, the mayor scheduled a public luncheon in her
honor.

What had especially surprised the community in
her little town northeast of London was that Mrs.
Springer had been notoriously incompetent at the
plane identification course, in fact never succeeding,
no matter how frequently she was tested, in passing
the critical test. But her instructor had finally relented,
and resignedly looked to one side when he authorized
her as a plane-watcher. Now, as he smiled and looked
at Mrs. Springer, standing to receive her tribute and
the aluminum cup, a councilman who knew of her
problems in class indulged himself to ask the question,
in front of the admiring assembly: How had she managed to know that it was indeed a Messerschmitt 210?
She beamed proudly and gave the narrative of her
analysis. You see, she explained, during all those hours
I spent staring at those wooden models, there was only
one of them that had a pilot in the cockpit, and that
was the Messerschmitt 210. So when I saw that the
plane that flew overhead *had a pilot flying it* I knew it
must be a Messerschmitt 210.

I tried that story out on my teacher, who found it
singularly unamusing. My roommate consoled me by
reminding me that our teacher found everything in life
unamusing. But finally, after arduous effort, I passed

the test, and spent a half-dozen nights staring at the skies over Dutchess County, performing my community service, which had suddenly graduated to national, even international, service.

Of which there was more: the war had sucked up most of the agricultural workers, and there was a huge apple crop to be plucked. Since this was a commercial enterprise we were assuaged to learn officially that we would be compensated, at the rate of twenty-five cents per hour; and to learn unofficially that no school monitor would notice if we smoked cigarettes while doing our duty. It was difficult to weigh the enormous pleasure of a few cigarettes against the stunning tiresomeness of holding with your left hand the stem of the apple, and with your right hand twisting the apple free, to deposit it in the huge basket at the bottom of the ladder. Since apple picking was volunteer community service, I soon gave it up, returning to my Strong Box, to puzzle over little imbalances in the ledger.

The headmaster had adopted as his school's motto *Non sibi sed cunctis*—"Not for oneself, but for all"; for the community. I was put off, in my teens, by the putative theory of the whole thing, thinking it faintly collectivist in nature. I suspected that the undeciphered motivation of the headmaster was really that, his school being attended, for the most part, by

sons of affluent Americans, a dose of communal work
would do them good, even as dishwashing in the army
serves as a great leveler before upwardly mobile soldiers get around to earning stripes or a gold bar. It was
thirty years after graduating from my school that I
realized that our headmaster (his name is—yes, he
lives, at age ninety-one—Edward Pulling) was on to
something.

Consider, in passing, social enterprises already in
place, especially those that have outlasted the season's
whim. The most widely referred to is, of course, the
Peace Corps, through which, since Mr. Kennedy announced its formation in 1961, 121,000 people have
passed. Most of its graduates remain enthusiastic
about the work they did, and the memory of it appears
to linger. The cost of maintaining the average Peace
Corps member has averaged $16,000 per year.

VISTA (Volunteers in Service to America) is generally thought of as a kind of domestic Peace Corps.
The idea was to mobilize volunteers for one year's
antipoverty service. The program, primarily because
of limited funding, never had more than a few thousand volunteers and during the Reagan Administration
was cut back, a reduction prompted not only by a concern for spending but by a reaction to charges of
politicization. Moreover, VISTA volunteers, in the

opinion of the Administration, were here and there making common cause with legal aid activists and other special-interest lobbying groups. VISTA attracted people older than those who went into the Peace Corps, the median age of its volunteers being thirty-five in 1983.

The California Conservation Corps, begun under Governor Reagan, was expanded under Governor Brown, and again under Governor Deukmejian. Its success is generally attributed to the leadership of B. T. Collins, an ex–Green Beret who lost an arm and a leg in Vietnam and did not return from Southeast Asia to America in order to suffer fools gladly. He gave the organization a motto ("Hard work, low pay, miserable conditions") as also a set of rules ("No booze, No dope, No violence, No destruction of state property, No refusal to work"). Needless to say such a regimen generated a considerable dropout rate (only one third of those who joined the program completed a year. The Collins Rule of rehabilitation? If you drop out, you may not apply for reentry). Reveille is at five, a "quiet hour" begins at ten P.M., and lights go out at eleven. An interesting requirement: Every member of the California CC is required to write something every day; mostly, these have been journals of the day's activities. The design is to teach young people how to express themselves, how to externalize their thoughts in writing, the better to equip them to handle their

work and their lives after leaving the California CC.
The work has been mostly ecological in nature; that,
plus maintenance of public places. In the opinion of
Professor Moskos, "the California Conservation Corps
stands as a preeminent example of how a comprehensive national-service program might operate at the
state level." The cost, in 1986, was $19,000 per vol-
unteer.

The Guardian Angels are the most prominent social warriors, obviously because of their dashing, self-
imposed mandate, which is to try to make travel in
New York City—i.e., walking, as well as subway and
bus riding—safe. This is a Sisyphean challenge. Although the Guardian Angels have numbered, cumu-
latively, eighteen thousand young men and women,
and have made over 4,300 citizen arrests, crime continues to rise, in large part under the stimulus of rising
drug consumption. The Guardian Angels are steeped
in controversy: New York policemen don't like them
(they are thought to be undisciplined amateurs);
public-interest lawyers don't like them (they are ac-
cused of slighting the civil liberties of their targets).
Yet no one has leveled a charge of corruption against
an organization whose annual budget is an exiguous
eighty thousand dollars, or forty dollars per active
member. For several years, proffered grants were re-
jected no matter from whom, on the grounds that the
organization (dominated by Lisa and Curtis Sliwa) did

not want to surrender its autonomy, which is total. The
makeup of the Guardian Angels is heavily black and
Hispanic; about a quarter are female. They go about
unarmed, of course, but they are trained in self-
defense and in the use of handcuffs.

The list of these and other ongoing social enterprises is lengthy. That long list is testimony both to the
existence of a large pool of potential volunteers, and
to a certain spirit-on-the-loose, drawn to the general idea of service in the public good wedded to self-
service in character building, in training, and in civic-
mindedness. In Atlanta's public high schools, community work is a graduation requirement. In 1987,
California passed legislation ordering the state university system to "urge" students to volunteer thirty
hours of community service every year.

Meanwhile, what kind of work do eighteen-year-
olds who do not go to college do? The March 1988
census gives the following breakdown of where
eighteen-year-olds find work.

	Percentage
Agriculture/Mining	3.8
Construction	3.9
Manufacturing	9.7
Transportation	1.3
Communications	0.5

Public Utilities	0.1
Wholesale and Retail Trade	51.4
Finance, Insurance, Real Estate	2.9
Services	25.9
Government	0.5

Manifestly, the majority live at home (where else?—on a salary between $5,500 and $7,500), working (the majority) in wholesale and retail trade.

Let's then ask: What work might usefully be done by these 1.6 million eighteen-year-olds without dwelling on how much training would be required to equip them to do such work? The gross figures given by Richard Danzig and Peter Szanton* of useful work that might be undertaken by young men and women of that age show that U.S. education could use the services of 1.2 million eighteen-year-olds, preferably those who have studied in high school, though it is not disqualifying if they didn't graduate. You don't need a high school diploma to help with school maintenance or even with order. Add to these:

Health	750,000
Child Care	820,000
Environment	165,000

(Under "Miscellaneous Services")

* In their 1986 book *National Service: What Would It Mean?*

Justice	250,000
Libraries and Museums	200,000
All Other	100,000
For a total of	3,485,000

A quick reading of the profile above tells us, then, that there are over twice as many national service openings as could be filled if 100 percent of our eighteen-year-olds who do not go on to college were to sign on. But would there be enough openings that did not require more education of the trainee? At this point two conclusions seem safe. The first is that fewer (at the beginning, far fewer) than 50 percent of eighteen-year-olds at large would enroll. The second: from the huge number (3,500,000) of openings, there would be more than enough slots for those who did.

There is much ebullience and energy in the scattered national service lobbies, exhibited in the spontaneous proliferation of enterprises that would qualify as chapters of National Service if national service were, so to speak, national policy. A typical journalistic paragraph from *Business Week* (October 24, 1988) reads: "Five days a week in cities and towns across the nation, 7,000 clean-cut young people meet for early morning calisthenics. Samuel Sampson, 18, follows push-ups and jumping jacks with a job building play equipment for San Francisco kids. Three thousand miles away, in Atlanta, Catherine Herbert, a 25-year-old high

school dropout, sets to work rehabilitating a vandalized
housing project. In Manhattan, former stock boy Earl
Ford, 19, begins delivering food to homebound old
people."

The variety of what is going on, much of it orig-
inating in the last few years, is impressive. Youth Service America is a genial and enterprising informational
omnipresence whose leading figure, Roger Landrum,
is resolute in resisting the notion that, in order to function, national service needs to be compulsory. The organization seeks to coordinate the activities of those
interested in nurturing the idea of national service and
to provide useful advice. It stresses the variety of the
work waiting to be done and the great untapped resources of the republic. One list of service-shy groups
and situations widely circulated by Youth Service
America in 1984 began with "Older Americans" and
retailed the datum from the General Accounting Office
that between 125,000 and 300,000 of the elderly "now
in nursing homes could be allowed to live in the normal
community if such services were available to them" as
could be provided by organized volunteers. "Overall,
more than two million elderly, mentally retarded, and
physically handicapped individuals are in need of
home assistance."

That same list goes on to describe twenty-five activities in which national service volunteers might usefully participate. It has the bracing effect of sharpening

the sensibilities as we survey needs some of which are obvious and of some of which we were—I was—quite simply, unaware . . .

- *Mentally and Physically Handicapped*: "Many of the same needs as the elderly but also with [special] needs such as reader services for the blind."
- *Education-related Activity*: "Perhaps the area of greatest need and opportunity . . . [The need is] for young volunteers to serve as remedial tutors in basic skills for schoolchildren."
- *Day Care for Children*: "There is a great need . . ."
- *Voter Registration*: "[It is] . . . possible to include transportation services on election day, if such service could be provided on a nonpartisan basis." (Youth Service America does not pause over the question of whether it serves the republic to expedite voting by the lackadaisical. If the service were directed to the handicapped eager to vote but unable to get to the polls, it would be a different matter.)
- *Volunteer Citizen Patrols*: ". . . neighborhood watch programs . . ." (The most celebrated citizen patrol is of course the Guardian Angels, described above.)
- *Library Work*: ". . . re-shelving and cataloguing [and] distributing books to people who are bedridden or otherwise secluded."
- *Energy Conservation Aid*: The need is for "energy

audits" and to "help install weatherization, etc."

- *Parks and Maintenance*: ". . . care for parks." The planting of gardens, the restoration of "forgotten parks and cemeteries."
- *Parks-Recreation*: ". . . summer camps or swimming instruction."
- *Community Cleanup Drives*: ". . . anti-litter campaigns."
- *Walk-a-thons*: "Young people are particularly well suited to raise money for charities through walk-a-thons."
- *Drug Education*: ". . . instruct young children on the danger of drugs."
- *Big Brother/Big Sister Programs*: " 'Adopt' children from broken homes."
- *International Family Adoption*: ". . . 'adopt' a newly entered family or individual from another country to help their adjustment to the U.S. . . . work with churches and other groups that provide information and necessities at the time of the swearing-in ceremony."
- *Outreach Programs*: ". . . distribute information regarding available private and public programs for people in remote parts of communities, or people who cannot easily leave their homes."
- *Snow-Removal/Emergency Aid*: ". . . work to help others, particularly older people . . ."
- *Painting of Buildings/Beautification*: ". . . paint or

repair churches and other private or public buildings."

- *Health Care*: ". . . visit hospital patients or those recuperating in their homes."
- *Orphanage Programs*: ". . . 'adopt' orphans and take to the zoo, for walks or visits, etc."
- *Arts/Cultural/Museums*: ". . . fund-raising, maintenance, leading tours, etc."

Since it isn't my purpose here exactly to dovetail the volunteer with the specific work to be performed in national service, I say only that it is plausible to assume that the republic could find untrained workers to do work our society would profit from seeing done, and that in order to perform that work the volunteer need not undergo training so extensive as to use up a significant amount of the year allotted to national service. Accordingly, I settle on the synecdoche, abstracting it from the researches of Messrs. Danzig and Szanton, who undertake to answer comprehensively the question, "Just what would all those people do?" I restrict myself to one paragraph from the generous space they devote to health care:

> The analysis of the health service sector conducted for this project by Dr. Phillip Lee and others concluded that tasks would vary greatly, depending on the type of institution to which NSPs [National Service Partici-

pants] were assigned and their own levels of skill, interest, and maturity. In inpatient facilities, for example [National Service volunteers] might provide information and referral, transportation, groundskeeping and maintenance, telephone reception, health education, child supervision, and recreation and craft activities. As Lee and his colleagues note, the level of supervision in many inpatient facilities is high, especially in larger hospitals, so a substantial fraction of the less mature and less capable [volunteers] might provide some of these functions. Nursing homes present a special opportunity because much of their work is performed by service employees rather than by professionals.

There follows an impressive table (page 27) entitled *"Estimated Number of [National Service Volunteer] Positions in Health Sector, by Health Setting."*

It amply serves our purposes here to reproduce the divisions and the estimated number of eighteen-year-olds who could do useful work, full-time, in these divisions:

Inpatient Care

Hospitals	77,500
Nursing Homes	87,300
Hospices	24,000
Mental Retardation Facilities	2,000
Mental Illness Facilities	2,300
Other Facilities	3,000
(Subtotal)	196,100

Ambulatory Care

Outpatient Facilities	12,000
Health Departments	23,000
Alcoholism Treatment	5,500
Drug Abuse	5,000
Community Mental Health	6,000
(Subtotal)	51,500

Home Care

Home Health Care	270,000
Meals on Wheels	112,500
Escort and Transportation	56,000
(Subtotal)	438,500

Other Health Services

Voluntary Associations	13,200
Research, Planning, etc.	16,000
(Subtotal)	29,200
Total	715,300

Equivalent projective work can be done—indeed, has been done, by Messrs. Danzig and Szanton—in the field of education, in which there are opportunities for an enormous number of volunteers (1,200,000); and then Child Care (820,000); Environment (165,000); Justice (250,000); Libraries and Museums (200,000). Most people who think about it know intuitively that the work is there to be done.

Consider one current affliction, eloquently identified by Moskos. He writes of the incurable mental disorder that causes deterioration of the memory and reasoning abilities. Alzheimer's disease afflicts about 5 percent of Americans over sixty-five years old and 20 percent of those over eighty. Some two million Americans have the disease. Its direct costs are estimated at $20 billion. The indirect costs may be much greater. The need for constant care places severe emotional burdens on relatives. Just to give family members a *temporary* break from caring for an Alzheimer's victim, either through home visits or adult day-care centers, would be a major help. Even a small corps of servers specializing in Alzheimer's care would provide immeasurable relief to very depressed families. There is no reason to suppose that even relatively affluent sufferers from Alzheimer's disease, let alone their families, would be less grateful for the occasional relief that might be provided by national service volunteers.

With Alzheimer's, unhappily, we only touch the larger problem. "Already by 1989, American families were paying [as noted] $20 billion a year for nursing homes out of their own pockets with an equivalent amount coming from the taxpayer," Mr. Moskos summarizes, and the results are sobering. Of couples with one spouse in a nursing home, half become impoverished within six months of admission; 70 percent of single elderly patients reach the poverty level after only thirteen weeks. It is hardly suggested that economic problems that drastic can be made to go away by national service. But they can be alleviated; and as already noted, volunteers can bring out of nursing homes, back to private quarters, hundreds of thousands of the elderly. If, while effecting relief for the elderly, we continue to focus on the primary objective, which is the moral well-being of the volunteers, much is accomplished.

☆   ☆   ☆   ☆   ☆   ☆   ☆   ☆   ☆   ☆   ☆

Arguments and Inducements

*T*his, I think, is the appropriate moment to reproduce (substantially) four pages I wrote in the book *Four Reforms* (New York, Putnam's, 1973) seventeen years ago. The fragment is relevant to a final section of this essay, in which I'll weigh in on alternative approaches to launching a program of national service. A short stretch of thinking done almost a generation ago is perhaps also interesting for cultural reasons, a minor historical benchmark in the evolution of one citizen's views toward the idea of national service. They reveal, in a useful way, the ideas I then had in respect of sanctions. The 1973

approach remains paradigmatic, but clearly it is over-
ruled by experience.

> And then [I wrote, in a book that dis-
> cussed at some length what I designated as
> the four principal domestic problems of the
> seventies: Welfare, Taxation, Education, and
> Crime] there is the question of the aged.
>   Mr. James Michener says it bluntly, that
> in his opinion the problem of caring for the
> aged looms as the principal social problem of
> the balance of this century: greater than eco-
> logical asphyxiation, greater than overpopu-
> lation, greater than the energy crisis. The
> figure is, I suppose, a product of scientific
> impressionism, but it has been said that one
> half of those who are now sixty-five years or
> older would be dead if medical science had
> been arrested even a generation ago. It is ab-
> solutely predictable that medical progress will
> continue, and with it the successes of ger-
> ontology.
>   Already it is a subject one shrinks from
> dwelling upon—the years and years [that go
> by] between the time when men and women
> are, if the word can be used in this context,
> ripe to die, and the day that increasing mil-
> lions will die. Euthanasia, pending word to
> the contrary from the Supreme Court, is un-
> thinkable. The cost of caring for the aged,
> most of whom need supervisory medical at-
> tention on a continuing basis, is suggested by
> this recent datum, namely, that the daily cost
> of a semiprivate hospital room in New York
> City is now over one hundred dollars [by 1990

the figure had more than doubled]. Good private homes for the aged are beyond the reach
of any except the very very few. There are
charitable and religious homes that will take
in elderly people in return for their Social
Security checks. But these—I think, for example, of the Mary Manning Walsh Home
in New York City—are necessarily exclusive,
with facilities cruelly unequal to the task at
hand.

The physical facilities and professional
services needed for the aged are extremely
expensive, and there is no way to avoid the
capital cost of them. Certainly there is no reason to discourage the private sector from ad-
dressing itself as vigorously as possible to the
building of suitable homes. Professional
medical aid will have to be furnished by doctors and highly trained nurses, the cost of
whose services is high, and will probably get
higher.

The only variable is in the cost of unskilled labor. And the only human leaven
is youth, whose functional companionship
could greatly affect the quality of the last
years.

The Mary Manning Walsh Home in New
York employs full-time forty doctors and
forty-three registered nurses. The cadre of its
professional staff is fifty. It employs, as cooks,
waiters, janitors, nurses' assistants, elevator
operators, laboratory workers, a total of 311.
There are 347 beds in the home, so that the
ratio of unskilled employees per patient is
very nearly one for one. Or, taking the figures
for the nation, in 1969 there were 850,000

Americans in nursing homes that employed 444,000 people, or one employee for 1.9 patients. (In 1963, there were 491,000 resident patients of nursing homes, so that in six years the figures almost doubled.)

The republic faces a crisis of a very particular and very poignant kind. We are aware of the reasons why less and less the aged die at home. The principal reason is the lengthening life span. Another is the need for certain kinds of care that cannot readily be provided at home. Another is the diminishing domestic utility of the great-grandmother or great-grandfather. Still another is the very high cost of urban living quarters where, now, 73 percent of the American people live. All of these combine to create the institution of the nursing home.

Simultaneous with the increase in the aged is the increase in the college population. That population in 1930 was 1.1 million. In 1970, 8.4 million. [By 1990, it had become 13.2 million.]

It is my proposal that the burden of the nonprofessional work [Professor Martin Anderson should pay attention to this qualification] done in behalf of the aged should be done by young men and women graduated from high school, during one year before matriculating at college. The idea of public service of some kind or another by the citizenry has frequently been proposed. There has been an instinctive coolness towards the idea primarily because of the conscriptive feel of it: the suggestion that government require anyone to do anything of a philanthropic char-

acter tends to put one off, and for reasons not
by any means all bad. The opportunity is great
for initiative from the private sector.

I envision a statement by the trustees of
the ten top-rated private colleges and universities in the United States in which it is
given as common policy that beginning in
the fall semester of 1976 (to pick a year far
enough away to permit planning, soon
enough to generate excitement), no one accepted into the freshman class will be matriculated until after he has passed one year in
public service. I say public service because if
the plan were very widely adopted, there
would be more young help available than
could be absorbed in the nursing homes
alone. There are many other ways in which
the young could be used. As [aides] in the
grade schools, just to give a single example
(there are 1,700 auxiliaries in the New York
schools alone), but for convenience I dwell on
the care of the aged.

As regards the financing, it would be required only that the government exclude this
category of volunteers from the provisions of
the minimum wage. Otherwise the economic
advantage would substantially dissipate. The
nursing homes would of course provide board
and pocket money (mostly, the volunteers
could continue to live at home). In the unusual case where the eighteen-year-old is
helping to support his own family, the college
could either suspend the requirement or con-
cert with foundations to find ways to permit
the young volunteers to eke out the year.

The colleges would take the position

that they desire, in matriculating freshmen, an earnest of public concern, and extra-academic experience of a useful kind. The intervention of hundreds of thousands of eighteen-year-olds into the lives of the aged would serve more than merely the obvious purposes of cleaning the rooms and pushing the wheelchairs and washing the dishes. It would mean, for the aged, continuing contact with young, spirited people in their most effusive years. For the young it would mean several things. It would postpone by a year their matriculation at college. College administrators are all but unanimous in their conviction that an older student, one year, rather than freshly graduated, from high school gets more out of college. [Indeed, most of the nation's business schools decline admittance to applicants freshly graduated from college. Their desideratum, beyond brains, is some time of practical, "real world" working experience.] The experience would, moreover, interrupt the inertial commitment to [just] more-and-more education, and some of the less strongly motivated, the rhythm having been broken, would probably elect not to go on to college. The experience—particularly because of the voluntary aspect of it—would remind young people at an impressionable age of the nature of genuine, humanitarian service, which is the disinterested personal act of kindness, administered by one individual directly to another individual. And the experience would touch the young, temperamentally impatient with any thought of the other end of the life cycle, with the reality of old age; with the human side of the detritus

whose ecological counterparts have almost
exclusively occupied fashionable attention in
recent years. Their capacity to give pleasure
to others, without the stimulant of sex, or the
pressure of the peer group, or the sense of
family obligation, or the lure of economic reward, could not help but reinforce the best
instincts of American youth, and these instincts are unstimulated at our peril. What it
might provide for society as a whole, this
union of young and old, is, just possibly, the
reestablishment of a lost circuit: of spirit, and
affection, and understanding.

I was told that one of the two boards of overseers
at Harvard deliberated my proposals. I have not established that this is so, or even whether, if the board
indeed did so, it was in bemused contemplation of a
wildly impractical proposal. Whatever: the private sector has not shown itself disposed to take action to
launch national service. Such action as has been taken
by the private sector has been in support of individual
programs; or, as with Youth Service America, administrative action designed to coordinate national service
activity. In any event, voluntary social action hasn't
sufficed. Enter the state, with its large inventory of
sanctions (". . . the provision of rewards for obedience,
along with punishments for disobedience, to a law;
remunatory, as distinguished from *vindicatory*, or *re-
muneratory*, *sanctions*," O.E.D., 2b.).

The obvious alternative, of course, is universal

compulsion. As things stand in America, apart from emergency military service, schooling is the only affirmative activity that is universally compelled.

The state—or, more properly, the several states, i.e., all fifty, and the District of Columbia—requires that everyone attend school and that those schools be "free" in that their expenses are paid for by city and county and state revenues. They are "free" to the parents except of course to the extent that the parents are themselves simultaneously contributing to the revenues of the city, county, and state. It is a fixed commitment of society that ten to twelve years of schooling is at least desirable and probably necessary to the development of well-functioning citizens.

Once the student is out of school, does the state have the authority, so to speak, to conscript youth for extra-military duty? The very constitutionality of any such proposal has been challenged in the disputatious literature of national service though not, in my judgment, persuasively. If, under the Constitution, states can require students to attend schools, and if local boards can specify the curriculum of those schools, then it would seem merely an extension of this gestational authority of the state over the aspirant citizen to impose such other training as the state, which is the agent of its citizenry, deems necessary fully to qualify him as a fellow member. As noted, it was until quite recently agreed that no citizen who could not read or

write would be permitted to vote. John Stuart Mill, the
great bard of the universal franchise, believed that no
citizen should be permitted to vote who had become
an economic ward of the state—to use modern language, no citizen on welfare should be permitted to
vote. The argument that it is unconstitutional for the
state, should its citizens determine upon its advisabil-
ity, to draft the entire eighteen-year-old population for
the purpose of finally qualifying it for fully active and
fully rewarded citizenship is difficult to make, and certainly cannot be made by citing any explicit constitutional prohibition.

However, prudential arguments against con-
scripted national service are entirely convincing.

Even if there are no constitutional barriers, there
are other problems. To begin with, we are no longer
dealing with human beings of an entirely malleable
age. It is hard enough, we learn from complaint after
complaint coming in from the inner cities, to force
twelve-year-olds who are determined not to do so to
attend school. It is easier to deal with refractory twelve-
year-olds than with eighteen-year-olds. Young children are not consulted on the question of whether they
should take instruction. One day, between the ages of
five and seven, they are taken to school and told to do
as directed. Moreover, it used to be routine, in such
societies as Stalin's, Hitler's, and Mao Tse-tung's, to
tell eighteen-year-olds what to proceed to do: to con-

tinue with their schooling, to report for duty at a state farm, to join the army or the secret police; whatever. A society whose traditions call for progressive freedoms of choice for young people growing up, leading to dramatic freedoms at age eighteen (the right to vote, the right to marry without the consent of the parents), has special problems in prescribing for the eighteen-year-old.

The state should not be given the authority to exact from unwilling citizens work they are not disposed to do, especially not under the general rubric of charity, even if the state reserves the right to specify under what circumstances full citizenship is earned. When cooperation with a collective goal is essential—in the event of war, or natural catastrophe—conscription is in order. The churchgoer instinctively reacts against requiring his neighbor to attend services, but is not for that reason any less zealous to evangelize. And a society advanced enough to be guided by libertarian presumptions should not exercise authority even while retaining a right to do so. Better that its citizens discover for themselves the special satisfactions that come to those who, by making a social-civic contribution, experience the subtle exaltation of community service.

So then: We reject compulsory national service, while desiring a heavily subscribed national service. In order to achieve this we are going to have to talk about sanctions/inducements. The individual citizen will make the calculations and come to his own decision. But the state is not for that reason bound to neutrality. The state need not forswear an active role in devising inducements.

Most frequently mentioned is the outright cash gift. The bill introduced at the beginning of 1989 by Senators Nunn et al. provides a ten-thousand-dollar subsidy toward higher education, except that if the National Service graduate doesn't want to spend it on education, he can draw it down for other purposes (e.g., a home mortgage). A novel proposal is substantially examined by Danzig and Szanton in their book, namely that Americans who decline to participate in national service should be made to pay a surcharge of 5 percent on their income tax. This is a dangerous road to travel, since the power to tax is indeed the power to destroy. A society that breeds legislators and pundits inventive enough to travel from an extension of the G.I. Bill for subscribers to national service to a proposed surcharge directed against the class of dissenters is obviously capable of coming up with a wide inventory of carrots and sticks.

The idea of rewarding the military veteran is no longer new. Moreover, the veteran need not have engaged in strictly military activity. In 1946 we spent one percent of our gross national income on the G.I. Bill. In current numbers, this is the equivalent of fifty-three billion dollars. Although there was no anticipation, in

1947, of any need for a large military, President Harry Truman came out strongly in that year in favor of what was called Universal Military Training, and one of the arguments used on its behalf was that George Washington had been in favor of it. President Truman did not prevail; in part, if I remember, because he was over-fond of mentioning the obvious advantages that had inured to him from service in the military, and didn't all Americans wish that their sons might be more like Harry Truman?

Still, the preconception that a "veteran" can only be someone who has been trained to aim bullets at potential aggressors isn't immutable. It was inconceivable, a generation ago, that women might one day be permitted to go to war, let alone that they should be drafted; but not long ago a constitutional amendment bounced about state capitols with widespread backing, which among other things would not have permitted discrimination against women going into the trenches. It is likely that, just as certain privileges have inured exclusively to veterans of the military in the past, similar privileges will in the future inure to veterans of a different order. Indeed, in the Peace Corps we seem to have come halfway: A graduate of the Peace Corps qualifies for government patronage not available to graduates of training programs run by Coca-Cola or IBM.

If, then, it is admissible that the state should seek

out means by which to distinguish between those who
acknowledge a civic debt and then participate in national service and those who do not, what might such
means be? Anyone who can contemplate a 5 percent
income tax surcharge can with equanimity contemplate civil discrimination against the dissident class by
any means that do not run afoul of the Constitution.
Caution is in order.

A better focus would be on society's acknowledging the sacrifices, and the civic-mindedness, of its first
class citizens. And one rewarding way to do this is via
a tax credit. This ought to be preferred to cash subsidies
of the kind advocated in the Nunn bill because the
economic health of a society depends on productivity.
A straight cash benefit can be abused. A tax credit
presupposes productivity, in the absence of which there
is nothing against which to apply a tax credit. (Yes,
special arrangements would need to be made for the
National Service graduate who never earns enough
money to owe a federal tax.)

Other means of linking citizenship to reward
are easy to imagine. I propose to paraphrase some
of the sanctions available to the government, and mentioned here and there in the literature, while defer-
ring for a few minutes my own judgment on those
I deem appropriately used to promote national
service.

One such means, proposed by numerous advocates of national service, is to link eligibility for certain subsidies and benefits to participation in the program. The principal dispenser of subsidies in the United States is of course the federal government. In grants for post-secondary school education, the government is generally thought of as helping the poor at the expense, obviously, of the less poor, and in many cases this is in fact what is going on. There are of course confusions, as when a federal grant, or loan, helps to pay for the higher education of a young American who, in virtue of that higher education, will predictably come to rest in an economic stratum above that of many taxpayers who helped him through college. Whatever the provenance of federal money, that it is distributed so abundantly among college students makes it obvious bait to influence young men and women of ripe age to perform national service. Indeed the idea of restricting federal aid to National Service graduates is, as we have seen, the "linchpin" that led Mr. Moskos away from favoring compulsory service, to crafting the Nunn bill, which specifies voluntary service.

There is a document called "The Federal Catalog of Domestic Assistance." It has over a thousand pages listing forms of direct federal domestic assistance available in many cases to everyone, in other cases to restricted groups—veterans, say, or wards of a single parent, or single parents. The following possibilities arise:

- What about denying some—or all—of these subsidies to persons who have not participated in national service? We pass over, for the moment, the question of by what age is it reasonable that national service should have formally been exercised, or how, thereafter, to redeem a delinquency: for the moment, consider only the question, Would we be willing to deny, say, federal financial aid to any student who does not sign up for national service at some point?

- Approximately half of full-time college students receive federal aid to help pay their tuition. Should a student be permitted to apply for federal aid if he does not sign up for national service? (A male student is not now permitted to apply for federal aid unless he has registered for the draft, as required by law. About 500,000 Americans have refused to register, or else have forgotten to do so. Presumably they foreswear federal aid. Either that, or else the law is not being enforced.)

- A "federal tax expenditure" is a verbal formulation I have always distrusted, but it is nevertheless used. What it isolates is that money lost to the Internal Revenue in virtue of exemptions given to a taxpayer, for whatever reason—dependents, depreciation, interest payments, etc. The list is not as long as it was before the 1986 tax law constriction, but it continues to add up to a sizable difference between taxable and non-taxable income. The citizen who failed to sign up for national service at age eighteen could lose the deduction privilege. This would not significantly affect an eighteen-year-old, unless he were a Steve Jobs wonder-boy type. But it would affect him progressively as he got older and forfeited the opportunity to take tax deductions. His penalties would, of course, reduce the quantity of federal tax expenditures.

- A surcharge of 5 percent in federal income tax has been suggested, as we have noted with distaste. Under the 1989 IRS code, this would have cost $113 per year to anyone making fifteen thousand dollars; $159 for anyone making twenty thousand dollars; $594 for those making fifty thousand dollars. What this amounts to is a negligible penalty for anyone moderately affluent, but I have warned against the (easily inflatable) discriminatory tax.

- The federal government guarantees deposits in banks and S&L's up to one hundred thousand dollars. Discontinue the guarantee to citizens who have not, by a certain age, signed up for national service?

- The government's largest group subsidy is to farmers. Should subsidies be denied to any farmer who by a certain age has failed to sign up for national service? Other occupational beneficiaries of government largess are everywhere, and modest fiscal needlework would stitch together laws and regulations that would adversely affect almost anybody.

- Social Security is now available to any American who works during his lifetime for forty quarters—i.e., a cumulative total of ten years. Should we add, to the required forty quarters of ordinary employment, national service, in order to qualify for Social Security? Already there is a positive bias, in that the government does not recognize voluntary work no matter how prolonged (or how taxing) in giving credits for Social Security. The housewife who spends twenty hours per week for fifty years doing philanthropic work is not acknowledged, under existing Social Security regulations, as earning her forty quarters required to qualify for Social Security. The problem of that lifelong volunteer is that she charged nothing for her charitable work. If she had been paid (however much), she'd have been logged into the Social Security system. A disturbing paradox.

- National service veterans might qualify for a rate of interest on student loans one half as large as that exacted from non-veterans, assuming that non-NS veterans were qualified to apply for such loans to begin with.

- For most sixteen-year-olds, the single most coveted franchise is a driver's license. Allowing for obvious exceptions (the sixteen-year-old is hired to drive an ambulance) should drivers' licenses extended at age sixteen automatically lapse at age eighteen, except on a showing that the young driver has signed up for national service?

As we get into the negative sanctions, we need to ask serious questions and post tough-minded, as well as benevolent, notes: Is youth really served by the progressively conventionalized presumption that he/she is king/queen of the walk? That it matters not what the young person does to earn the respect, as well as gratitude, of fellow citizens, including those who are older and who have carried the burdens and, often, done the duty of older people? A great arsenal of rights and perquisites and allurements and toys has been organized for the benefit of youth, and it has been questioned in recent times, in exploring questions other than the idea of national service, whether it does young people the good Americans wish for them to continue, reflexively, in the direction we have taken with respect to their growing years. In recent decades youth were given the vote at eighteen. Federal subsidies for higher education were born after the Second World War. What sometimes seems like the whole of the entertainment industry writhes to do their bidding. They can marry or not marry, have sex with or without the burden of children, conceive and bring children to term or abort them. Other than the psychological-emotional obstacles associated with puberty and adolescence, not very much is exacted of the average late-teens American approaching the twenty-first year. And it is incidentally to be noticed, but not dismissed, that the effort to universalize national service protects those who forthrightly aspire for such an experience but tend to be intimidated about undertaking it for fear of being charged with a kind of moral exhibitionism, a fear that causes some Mormons, for instance, quietly to change the subject if asked whether, as young people, they had done their missionary work.

The mind turns then, as in consideration of distributive justice one expects that it should, to marks of preferment, and one thinks of military veterans who have lifetime privileges redeemable at any veterans' hospital. In Connecticut, the first one thousand dollars of real property is not taxed if one is a veteran. That tree of preferment can bear a lot of fruit.

The list of possibilities is as long as the imagination is fertile, and its single intent is: to defer to citizens who have documented and demonstrated their gratitude to the society they live in—the society that protects them, their children, and the common patrimony. And which will cost the rest of us to give, too, and be grateful for doing so.

C H A P T E R   T E N

☆   ☆   ☆   ☆   ☆   ☆   ☆   ☆   ☆   ☆   ☆

Dollars and Cents

*W*e reach, inevitably, the question of financing. Most recently (at the Hoover Institution conference, referred to above) Professor Moskos fixed the cost at a handy one billion dollars per one hundred thousand enrollees—ten thousand dollars per person.

In his book he is more detailed. Historical figures inform us that for residential programs, defined as the participant living at home, costs will range from $13,000 (Michigan) to $19,000 (California); for non-residential programs, from $6,000 (Michigan) to $21,000 (Marin County). Where a particular program will fall within the spectrum depends largely on staff-

participant ratios. The level of enrollee compensation—below or above minimum wage—is a relatively
small factor (though workers' compensation and medical insurance are not). Judging from current opera-
tions, it seems that a well-run residential program
could be had for about $16,000 per person (what the
Ohio corps costs), while a non-residential program
based on the sponsor system would probably cost
$9,000. Settle for the Moskos ten-thousand-dollar
figure.

There are several reasons for resisting the natural
inclination to finance national service through the federal government. The first of these is economic, the
second psychological.

Although a moment's thought documents it, in
the great fiscal blur of the twentieth century we tend
to forget that no dollar is at the disposal of the federal
government that wasn't collected in the first instance
from someone who is a resident of one of the fifty
states; so that to speak of "federal" money is to speak
of an accumulation in Washington of moneys brought
in by taxing citizens who are residents of identifiable
states.

In *Four Reforms* I examined as of 1971 the net
effect on each state of the flurry of dollars that go to
Washington and then back ("round-trip dollars"). I
have brought these figures forward as far as is possible
(1988). In the Appendix, the figures are given under

the title "The Costs and Distribution of Federal Aid."
The states are listed in order of decreasing per capita
income, and ranked by per capita income. Then the
per capita income of the state is given; then the tax
burden of the state per dollar of grants from the federal
government; and, finally, the state's contribution to
federal taxes as a percentage of the whole. When considering a new national program it clearly makes sense
to ask whether we shouldn't jolt ourselves awake from
the myth of the spontaneously generated dollar sprout-
ing up in Washington, D.C., and then to be guided by
the skepticism appropriate to the question: What is the
point in the federal government's taxing one hundred
million dollars from Rhode Island, if the purpose is
to return to Rhode Islanders one hundred million
dollars?

For illustrative purposes we can pluck from the
chart in the Appendix the following: The average per
capita income of the states in 1988 was $16,444. The
number of states whose average income was that figure
or higher was seventeen. The number whose average
income was less than that was thirty-three. The more
affluent states, in theory, send money to Washington
on the understanding that a part of what they send
will be transferred to the less affluent states. But the
chart reveals that it does not always work in that way
(e.g., the state of Texas, with an average income of
$14,640, earned less per capita than the average state

and therefore, one would have supposed, received a net subsidy from the more affluent states. Yet the figures show that for every $1.31 sent to Washington, Texas got back only one dollar.

So then, one reason not to endorse federal financing is that federal financing is primarily a fiscal superstition, engaged in because it is so widely imagined by much of the voting public that dollars that come from Washington, as distinguished from dollars that flow to the state capitol from within that state's borders, are painlessly created, ventures in exnihilation.

But the primary reason for opposing federal funding for national service programs is to reinforce the indispensable initiative of the individual states.

It is one thing for the federal government to lend its power to the states, in measured proportions, intending to induce cooperation with national service— by withholding, for instance, post-secondary school loans from those college students who decline to subscribe to national service. Here the federal government is merely extending concrete moral aid to the individual states. But it is the states, a national program having been enacted, that should take the primary role in attracting volunteers to service, and thereafter they that should raise the money to pay the costs.

What kind of costs?

That depends on the activity an individual volunteer finds himself in.

Here are the variables: 1) How much money per week does the state pay the national service volunteer? 2) How much does the state pay the staff that administers the program? 3) How many of the volunteers live at home, how many, so to speak, on-site? And, 4) What kind of a bonus, if any, will the state pay the national service volunteer at the end of his tour of duty?

On these points a few observations, but first I quote the findings of Professor Moskos that lead him to his one billion dollars per ten thousand participants. He says that the average participant, based on his canvass of existing mini-programs, receives one hundred dollars per week ("enough money to buy food and transportation . . . and have a modest amount left over for personal needs"). Add health and life insurance and the figure rounds out at $6,500. If the participant has to live away from home, add $4,500 for room and board, but subtract from his stipend one thousand no longer needed for transportation—leaving you with the figure of ten thousand dollars per year ("about the cost of maintaining each individual enrolled in a Job Corps residential center").

Here are some ambient data by which we gain perspective.

- It costs the government $35,000 per year to maintain a soldier in the modern army.
- The cost of keeping an inmate in jail is about the same, $30,000 per year.
- VISTA volunteers cost an average of $13,000 per year.
- ROTC spends $5,000 per year (for four years) on each of its college students.

Now, nobody is going to be able definitively to establish that for every million dollars a state spends on a national service program the state a) is losing a million dollars; b) is losing less than a million dollars; or c) is going to wind up with a positive balance, more than a million dollars. Too many answers to too many questions have to be conflated to permit a responsible prediction.

Take, for example, the case of our Robert Ely, whose activities in the Owlwood Retirement Home have been touched on. He spent a forty-hour-week year (two thousand hours) in an old people's home. The promotional literature for national service is adamant in its insistence that no one is going to be displaced from his job by a NS participant; but of course this is not necessarily true. Maybe Robert did displace a low-paid hospital auxiliary. If so, did that auxiliary go on to unemployment? Or might it be that he went on to a higher-paying job, within the institution or outside it, yielding more taxes to the state? An unanswerable question. In any event, it challenges the dynamic of a free society to decline to hire someone at a lower wage because by doing so someone being paid a higher wage becomes supenumerary. To fall into that trap is the equivalent of supposing that a minimum wage is an effective economic weapon. It is impossible to find a creditable economist who believes this. Either the minimum wage is low enough to be meaningless, or else it is so high as to cause unemployment in low-income workers.

Another: If a society acknowledges an obligation, however unspecified, to take care of its elderly to the extent they are not satisfactorily cared for by private sources, then the state benefits to the extent that it is paying ten thousand dollars for Robert's services but receiving services from Robert which, were they purchased from the market, would cost the state more than ten thousand dollars—perhaps much more. If Robert is working at a privately run facility, then the value of his services contributes either to a diminution in the cost of running that facility (Who benefits from the reduced cost?) or else his services contribute to an enhancement in the quality of the service received by patients at that facility. Or a combination of the two. If the facility operates in a state that levies an income tax, then the patient (or the patient's sponsors), to the extent that costs decrease, deducts less money from his taxable income, marginally benefiting the state.

Consider another synecdoche, the national service volunteer who spends his/her time helping to keep a city clean, both by attending to the physical problem—removing trash—and by administering a program by which trash gets removed. The city gradually begins to glow a little, even as all Paris came to glow a little when Charles de Gaulle decided to clean up the city. What is the financial impact on the economy of a cleaner city?

The question is asked in all seriousness, denying attention only to those who step up apodictically to say that there is *no* effect of a financial character from a cleaner city. To say such a thing would require one to take the position that cleanliness has no bearing at all on the morale of a city's inhabitants or on its tourists, and this affronts common sense. Granted, people can get used to dirty surroundings even as they can get used to prison walls. But to say they can get used to trash does not answer the question: What happens when the trash is removed? Is there a perceptible quickening of the gait? Does the evangelistic impulse germinate, or heighten, to give care to other debris that tend to accumulate at the disconsolate corners of one's life? Do we end by caring more about conservation in general?

Or take a third example. Consider the national

service subscriber who spends his year performing one of the services, described earlier, one that relates to education. Tutoring young and not-so-young illiterates. And helping to maintain order—yes, the school equivalent of a bouncer in a bar: they are *desperately* needed. They stoke the morale by helping with otherwise neglected and, often for that reason, intimidating studies; they preside over study periods and generate the kind of tranquillity that gives the flighty mind that touch of specific gravity into which learning can unobtrusively tread. And they free the professional teachers to teach.

How do we measure the financial meaning of one thousand students engaged in such activity in the city of San Francisco? The figures are absolutely resolute on one point, namely that the farther one goes in schooling, the higher one's income is likely to be (up to a point, as acknowledged). The marginal contribution made by a ten-thousand-dollar national service volunteer who eases one or two or a dozen students out of illiteracy or who helps to promote that order and quiet that make undistracted study thinkable is not quantifiable. Speculation is legitimately unconfined, short only of the hypothesis that increased learning has no bearing at all on the financial life of the community. A state cannot bring in revenues except to the extent that its residents generate revenues, from which it follows that the state has a direct interest in individual domestic prosperity.

We come then to the principal question, which is, What are the likely long-term economic effects on the national service volunteer?

Here we must be careful, not only for reasons of statistical modesty, but because carelessness makes it possible to be hoist by one's own petard. If National Service volunteer Jane J. were so taken by the nature of philanthropic work that she resolved, after her year in the slums of San Francisco, to volunteer to work in a mission in Peru, it could indisputably be held that the State of California, by spending ten thousand dollars on young Jane, contrived to secure California's perpetual exclusion from any share in Jane's immediate future income, however exiguous. But while we are prepared to assume that the incidence of foreign missionaries is likely to increase in any country in which national service is institutionalized, it is not planned that national service should go into the business of producing missionaries. It is a very long road between the dead soul of the mass-man, ignorant of any sense of obligation, over to Mother Teresa, whose life is devoted to helping, as she puts it, the poorest of the poor. The person exposed to national service who will emerge a missionary will always be the exception.

The purpose of service is to rouse the civic sense. If that is done, never mind the saintly missionaries; society becomes among other things more durable— safer, lovelier, and more precious would be the easiest way to put it, if one is bound on finding a linkage with dollars and cents.

If (to live in a fantasy) all three million-plus young men and women at age eighteen were engaged in national service—i.e., if young people on turning eighteen all signed up—at ten thousand dollars each that would come to thirty-odd billion dollars, which is about 0.6 percent of the national income, less than we were paying for the G.I. Bill after the Second World War. Were such to happen it could very well turn out, as we have argued, that society in due course would one day be enriched by more than thirty billion dollars per year—as the G.I. Bill demonstrably enriched America more than it cost the government.

But of course we are talking about far less than 100 percent participation (at least for the foreseeable future). If we achieved 50 percent participation we'd be talking about sixteen billion dollars . . . as the typical liberal commentator would at this point put it, Less Than the Price of One Aircraft Carrier Group. I am allergic to exogamous comparative dollar figures, so widely used in workaday polemical chitchat *("For the cost of landing a man on the moon, we might have built one million one hundred and thirty-seven thousand and eight low-middle class dwelling units").* But I did not think it right to let the comparative figure go entirely ignored here; lonely, unobserved.

☆   ☆   ☆   ☆   ☆   ☆   ☆   ☆   ☆   ☆   ☆

A Call to Arms

*L*et us proceed to describe a plan whose essential design I endorse. Some of my proposals are also endorsed by authors of other models for a national service program.

Richard Danzig and Peter Szanton in their book anatomize four models of national service programs. The first is a school-based program, in which states would require a certain number of unpaid hours from high school seniors before they became eligible for a high school diploma. The second model is draft-based—a completely civilian national service as an alternative to military service. Model three is voluntary, building on existing philanthropic programs and government programs without significantly increasing existing incentives. The fourth (and final) model identified is universal service, a system in which a year of civil or military service is exacted of every citizen, with sanctions in the form of criminal penalties and tax surcharges. In addition to these four models, some analysts—e.g., James Strock, the Assistant Administrator for Enforcement in the EPA and formerly on the board of directors of Youth Service America—identify what they call "the Buckley model," based on the passage devoted to the subject in my book *Four Reforms*, substantially reproduced in Chapter 9—i.e., a program in which colleges and universities take the initiative by declining to accept applicants who have not served.

I have already submitted to second thoughts the so-called Buckley model. And I have given reasons for opposing the universal (or conscription-based) national service; the military-draft-based model; and the model that, though voluntary, is unreinforced by rewards and sanctions. The school-based model described by Danzig and Szanton is promising, but only as an element of a fifth model which I proceed to recommend and designate as the Service Franchise model while, along with Gladstone, awaiting a better term for it.

The word "franchise," in recent generations, has been restricted to the vote or to the licensing of retail outlets. In fact, the Oxford English Dictionary devotes whose directors should be volunteers (*their* national service?), appointed by the President with due concern to broaden the constituency of the program.

A vital function of the Administration would be to establish how long a participant would need to work in order to qualify for his certificate of service. The states decide what are the accrediting activities and which should be given precedence. But only a single agency can reasonably decide what the total contribution, measured in time served, ought to be.

The idea of one year's service appeals, one supposes, primarily because one year has the psychological impact of a life integer, even as one spends four *years* in college, and college students after one *year* go from being freshmen to sophomores and so on to juniors to seniors. One year should be the time span the NSFA should be concerned to institutionalize.

But the Administration would have the authority to permit arrangements other than consecutive, full-time, fifty-week service. What of the young man or woman eager to do national service but wishing to do it concurrently with college work—by, let us say, devoting two thousand hours over four years, or five hundred hours per year; at forty hours per week, the equivalent of three months per year? This accommodation could be done without trespassing on college calendar property: most colleges suspend work for three months during the summer. The alternative

should be authorized, always provided that the NSFA
was alert to evasions in the making—but here, except
in extraordinary circumstances of the kind mentioned
above, the state would be the accrediting agent. The
NSFA would govern only in that that agency alone
could agree to suspend the prohibition against federal
student financial aid by the federal government. It
would (should), as a matter of course upon receiving
the recommendation of the state branch, accommo-
date students desiring custom-made arrangements
There are students who routinely work many more
hours in a week than forty. There are the Stakhanovites
who might, in eight weeks rather than twelve, discharge their four-hundred-hour obligation. The NSFA
should always remind itself that its function is to assist
in the evolution of a national ethos and that it is entirely
in the spirit of American individualism to encourage
individuated programs, provided they are not primarily
evasive in design.

    3. Beginning with the promulgation of an NSFA
code, all federal financial educational aid would cease
for any student who did not have a certificate in hand
giving evidence that he was a veteran of national service, or was scheduled to serve soon, even as it ceases
today for any student failing to register for the draft.

    I have urged above what I deem a refinement in
the "rewards" system, as the psychologists use the
term. The Nunn bill speaks of ten thousand dollars

forwarded to the college of choice of the National Service graduate, tax free. Under the Service Franchise model, on the other hand, National Service graduates should be permitted immunity from the first ten thousand dollars owed to Internal Revenue. Under the Nunn alternative, a National Service graduate needs to do one of two things in order to walk into his reward: go to college, or buy a house. There is no reason to make the reward restrictive. And since anyone who chooses to do anything other than become a Carthusian monk is almost certain to pay taxes, the prospect of relief from ten thousand dollars in taxes is both real and appropriate—real because the sum of money is substantial, appropriate because the government is acknowledging a service done. I foresee, as already mentioned, the objection that the very poor are for all intents and purposes never taxed, especially after the comprehensive relief granted in the 1986 tax reform to the lower brackets. But the number of Americans who go a full lifetime without incurring any federal tax is insignificantly small. Any citizen who failed to engage in productive endeavor through a lifetime probably should not experience "relief" that would anyhow be supererogatory, given that citizens at that level are regular beneficiaries of state welfare payments.

For the sake of administrative convenience, the governing body, the NSFA, might stagger the rules

here, with the objective in mind of shuffling young
volunteers into the program other than in great one-
year generational batches. It might be prudent, for
instance, to rule that those born in 1973 would need
to do their service sometime before beginning junior
year, and would be free to apply for conventional federal aid as freshmen and sophomores; while those born
in 1974 would need to display their NSFA certificates
before matriculating as freshmen.

The denial of post-secondary school loans has no
force, needless to say, with full-time students who do
not seek federal loans (they are about one half of those
who go to college), whether it is because they don't
need them or because they don't qualify for them.
Those students who don't get federal loans but do get
loans from their colleges are easily reached by applying
sanctions on the colleges themselves—e.g., no college
that fails to expedite NSFA performance by its students
will qualify as a vehicle for federal grants. Here the
administrative machinery of the civil rights acts is relevant. In 1978 students at Grove City College were
disqualified by the courts from receiving federal grants
on the grounds that the college refused to sign com-
pliance forms for Title IX of the Higher Education Act
of 1972 which forbids sex discrimination. What can
be done to discourage sex discrimination can be done
to discourage civic neglect, apathy, etc. Students who
do not need aid of any kind are immune from this

particular sanction, even as during the Civil War for a considerable period of time people who could come up with three hundred dollars were immune from the draft. But it is not just the poor who are to be punished. We have mentioned the loss of a driver's license. John Cadwalader Abercrombie III would have a hard time playing the gay blade at school if he needed either a bicycle or a chauffeur. Not much more needs to be said on the point.

The financial aid sanction in question, as noted, is of course useless against the 1.6 million young people who will not be going to college in 1991 or 1992. These are less easily reached by the federal government, given that they rely, at that age, so little on government. It would hardly intimidate an eighteen-year-old to be told that his bank accounts will no longer be protected by the Federal Deposit Insurance Corporation. Few eighteen-year-olds, or for that matter twenty-one-year-olds, own and operate their own farms, relying for their economic survival on the government for farm subsidies. And for so long as the minimum wage is lower than the wage one has to pay in order to hire an hour of a productive eighteen-year-old's working time, tampering with the minimum wage intending to discourage non-volunteers is not an effective device. Moreover, it would be bizarre to use it in situations in which a primary objective is to persuade young people to work for one year at, in most cases, less than the minimum wage. Youth not bound for college would need sanctions exercised by individual states. These could include the denial of a driver's license—in most cases, the ultimate weapon.

4. Although the rights of the individual states to shape their own programs, specifying compensation and the like, should be preserved, the national aspect of the plan would fail if deviations were to become eccentric, particularly so if they were to do that to the point of luring young men and women either to a state that had synthetic national service programs, or away from a state that had only especially disagreeable programs. Having said this, obviously it is desirable that excesses of states be tamed, as to some extent they now are in taxation policies by citizens who register their dissent with their feet, moving their residence elsewhere. A state that moved too heavily in the direction of Sparta would begin to lose its mobile population to Athens.

But if we have in mind a national service program, it needs to be that, as distinguished from bizarre programs that appeal to states responding to bizarre lobbies, publicly desirable programs receive priority—e.g., care for the aged, over teaching children how to swim.

The reason for this is self-evident: The formal satisfaction felt by volunteers when their service is done should be keen, even as the formal stigma that would attach to those who shirk their duty should be felt keenly. But these experiences are unlikely if there is too great a blur around the kind of services performed. A plausible National Service Franchise Program would bind all the states to cooperation, on a showing of massive support by voters in those states for no-nonsense participation in the program. And the program having been approved by the individual states, its realization would be made possible by the appropriation of state money. And the infrastructure of state programs would be supported by the use of those sanctions of the federal government already discussed.

5. Beyond the question of federal loans proferred or withheld, the selection of appropriate auxiliary sanctions ought to be primarily the business of the individual state, even as, on the question of who should establish the criteria by which national service obligations are discharged, it is the states that should make the decision, within the boundaries established by the federal program. Granted that there will be some flimsy programs, even as in any college there is the "gut," or easy, course. The state is bound to crop up that will want to give credit for, oh, one hundred hours of television watching in order to explore ethnic bias; that sort of thing. The states should exercise workaday authority to license activities as qualifying for NSFA credit, and to assign priorities respecting what needs most to be done. In Florida, perhaps care for the old; in Wyoming, conservation; in Illinois, school tutoring;

in the District of Columbia, crime prevention. But probably the NSFA should be given the right, when let us say ten of its twelve members are agreed on the matter, to disqualify for credit any state program that appears to be outrageously circumventive of the whole idea.

And, of course, the federal government can put pressure on individual states, even as it applies pressure on the states in other matters—speed limits, drinking ages for minors, highway billboards. Then the national service idea can absorb an element of latitudinarianism, just as a first-rate college can get away with a few gut courses.

The National Service Franchise Administration might elect, as the program evolves, to recommend to Congress that it impose sanctions designed to prod the consciences of morally sluggish state legislatures. True, a few years' experience with national service might establish that there is no need for the federal government to goad the states, there being so much good to be done that serves everyone's purposes. But a huge array of incentives and sanctions is there to be used, should it be deemed useful and desirable, against refractory states. Obviously Congress is not going to impose sanctions unless the majority of Americans, expressing themselves through the House of Representatives, and the majority of the states, through the Senate, are determined to universalize the service. In the absence of a national political will, a national service program is fated to founder.

In reaching for intensified sanctions, we should rely on individual states to come up with their own.

Suppose, say, that the legislature of the State of California came to the conclusion that the time had come to transform the idea of national service from a desirable abstraction into a concrete requirement of effective citizenship. What might the state government routinely do in California to cultivate effective, contributory, creative citizenship?

Among other things, California requires attendance at high school, a diploma from which is a valuable credential for many who seek jobs. One sanction might be the denial of a high school diploma except to students who produce the qualifying certificate from the NSFA. This sanction should be examined and applied with care, inasmuch as it would hardly advance the objectives of national service to devise criteria for qualification which permitted boys and girls of exaggeratedly young age to discharge their obligations. Or to discourage anyone from finishing high school. Age sixteen should be the first year at which credits under the NSFA program can begin to be earned.

6. What about the 1.3 million eighteen-year-olds who go on to college?

While it is desirable that national student service

be performed before matriculation, to do national service while still at college is practical. There is already a substantial tradition of taking a junior year elsewhere, often abroad. Year Three could become the time in which the college student does his national service. We are talking now about twenty-year-olds, and their increased maturity and experience would not only make it easier to train them for more specialized work than that expected of eighteen-year-olds, there would be time, during the first two college years, to give special thought to the nature of national service work done, with the view to wedding it to the profession the student has in mind to pursue—doctor, lawyer, businessman, accountant, government worker, teacher. It could thus be compatible with internships, field work, etc.

There will be the student who, for reasons ranging from plausible to compelling, wishes to put off national service but does not want to risk forfeiting the benefits to be received on the strength of a pledge to national service. We are speaking about the student who says: For this reason and that, I am most anxious to continue in college without interruption for the next four years, but I pledge that the year after I graduate will be devoted to national service.

The state's National Service Board having accepted the student's bona fides, that student would continue to receive those benefits otherwise reserved for national service alumni. The question arises, What is to be done in the event of a subsequent default? And how do we reasonably define a default?

At age twenty-two, having graduated from college, student L.A.Z. Evader does not show up for duty, as he had promised to do. (We distinguish between him and the young man or woman who negotiates an extension with the National Service Board.) On the evader, the law would visit all the relevant sanctions. On the procrastinator, attenuated penalties. If by age twenty-five the volunteer has defaulted for three consecutive years, the law will judge him to be a delinquent, and while the sanctions will be ongoing—the same sanctions that would apply to those who had never volunteered for national service—the government will seek a return on those benefits already extended. Here one might study and learn from the history of the federal government's efforts to get from delinquents payments on money owed. We know that 18 percent, as of 1987, had defaulted on student loans. At first the government was indulgent toward the deadbeats, but as the dollar amount of such defaults rose (by 276 percent between 1983 and 1987), attitudes hardened, and it was decided, pursuant to the goals already stipulated in the Debt Collection Act of 1982, to try everything to satisfy delinquent debts: use private collection agencies, report delinquent debtors to com-

mercial credit bureaus, offset federal employees' sal-
aries, and withhold IRS tax refunds.

These and other such details do not engross us
and should not distract us. But a moment's thought
should be given to whether, and if so how, in later
years a delinquent might cure the record. Presumably
if, at age thirty-eight, he turned himself over to the
national service board and went out to serve for one
year, he would extirpate the default. It should be made
possible for him to regain his first-class citizenship by
doing something less than full-time work, because any
demand that exigent on a grown person occupied
professionally and probably also as a parent is an in-
ducement to live with the delinquency rather than to
effect exculpation. A strictly mathematical formula
would require the adult citizen to serve as many hours
as the eighteen-year-old did who worked full-time for
one year. At forty hours per week, the full-time volunteer did community service for two thousand hours.
To give that many hours of service, but over a period
of five or ten years, becomes manageable. Over ten
years, that comes to two hundred hours per year of
community service, or four hours per week, a half day.

It might prove desirable—experience will tell—to
increase the number of hours owed to national service
in proportion as one delays discharging that duty, so
that, let us say, at age forty the citizen might owe not

two thousand hours, but three thousand hours. Such variations are best experimented with. They too depend substantially for their success on the spirit generated by the entire enterprise. If successful, the citizen would a.) wish to serve, and b.) wish to reintegrate himself with his fellow citizens, born in 1973 or thereafter, measuring his delinquency not merely in terms of lost benefits, but lost self-esteem.

7. Is there any formal way in which to recognize what one might think of as further, postgraduate work in national service? Not really. If the program succeeds, then at age twenty-one the veteran, his certificate in his pocket, is not likely to forget that there are old, lonely people out there, families who need day care, illiterates who need coaching, streets that need cleaning, forest fires that need fighting. The last thing one would wish a national service program to promulgate is a regimented society, but it is not regimentation to attempt consciously to universalize a continuing concern for one's fellow men, a felt gratitude for those Americans, dead now, who passed along what we enjoy, in usufruct.

The idea of rendering service, we know already, isn't dependent on a national service program. If it were, there would be no civic work going on, as there is at present, when there is no formal service system. The program here proposed is the kernel of a national possibility, nurtured by an ongoing civic disposition, even as college is supposed to be the kernel of an ongoing attitude toward learning. If the idea takes hold, as one hopes that it will, the appetite to contribute to the health and morale of the republic would endure. Far from thinking themselves entirely discharged from showing interest in other people, and in other concerns, they would find their appetite stimulated, as noted, even as the aesthetic appetite is stimulated by early exposure to music and the arts. The satisfaction that comes from the discharge of an obligation gives life to the problem that was faced. If it was a military problem, the veteran understands the purpose of, and even the need for, a military. If one once kept company with a dying old woman, one knows that today another woman, who needs company, is dying. As veterans of national service, these graduates will have earned chevrons and their sense of involvement with the community will run deeper. It is after all only sensible to expect that a sense of solidarity with one's fellow citizens, a sharpened esprit de corps, will survive the initial term of service. Successive experiences would remind our Robert Ely, now a veteran of national service, of his status as a Citizen, First Class, even as a military veteran is from time to time reminded of his status long after the experience of service has been lost to recollection. Not so much in the service itself, then, as in the recall of service, engraved and re-engraved gently but insistently by a dozen burins, decade after decade, lodged in the moral memory.

Such mild but suggestive privileges—society's recognition of his status and of the service with which he has earned a place in his home—are welcome. A greater share of its patrimony would continually reinforce the awareness in the veteran's mind of his connection to the community, of his indebtedness to it, and, little by little, of its indebtedness to him.

EPILOGUE

☆   ☆   ☆   ☆   ☆   ☆   ☆   ☆   ☆   ☆   ☆

*T*eased a little wisecrack into the text back
there, at the expense of Harry Truman.
He was very proud of his service in the
army, during the First World War, and I remember a
reaction I and some of us had, as college students,
while he served as President, campaigning in favor of
universal military training and trumpeting his own experience as, perhaps, exemplary. I am impelled to reflect on the phenomenon, and once again it is best
examined autobiographically.

I entered college with eighteen hundred other students in the fall of 1946. The class was greatly swollen
because, ever since Pearl Harbor, Yale had grandly

promised every graduating senior from high school whom it admitted using admissions' conventional criteria that when the war ended, by hook or by crook Yale would make room for him. I do not know whether the trustees who made this commitment gave any thought to what would have been Yale's plight if the Second World War had gone on to Peloponnesian lengths. It was bad enough, with physical quarters constructed to receive six hundred students, to have to make room for eighteen hundred.

Happily, then, the overextension amounted to 200 percent, not 1,000 or 10,000 percent. Yale faced the problem by maintaining in service a few dozen hastily erected Quonset huts intended for use by student soldiers and sailors sent to New Haven for special training, and The Unfortunate of the class of 1950, the nonveterans, were sent there to live during freshmen year. The veterans (twelve hundred of the eighteen hundred) were handled with procrustean dispatch: All we had to do was double up. Where, before the war, a suite in Yale colleges (one living room, two bedrooms) was occupied by two students, now it was occupied by four. This proved quite tolerable to a body of men who, when last barracked, had expected anywhere from twenty to ninety human bodies to share the same roof.

I reflect on the extent to which lines were drawn between veterans of the war and apple-cheeked freshmen straight out of secondary school. At first the dif-

ference was marked primarily by dress: we veterans
were almost studiedly wedded to khaki pants. But after
a month or so, the non-veterans, following the lead of
their grizzled seniors, adopted similar dress, and,
really, it was not all that easy to stare into the face of
an eighteen-year-old and then a twenty-year-old and
discern in the latter the distinctive scars of service in
the military.

For one thing, there was no clear way, before the
days of the superdirectors of Hollywood who learned
exactly how to atrophy the youthful mien to convey
service in Vietnam, to distinguish between the features
of such as my roommate, who had taken part in the
invasion of Iwo Jima, his closest friend dying at his
side on the beach from machine-gun bullets, and such
as myself, who spent twenty-four months in U.S. training camps, the majority to be sure miserably uncom-
fortable, but the bullets we needed to dodge as we
crawled on our bellies under barbed wire were carefully aimed several feet above our rumps. Still, we were
all veterans. We had shared a large experience, and
those of us who had not been sent to combat duty were
simply lucky beneficiaries of entirely dispassionate
computers, or whatever they then used in their stead.

In part the indistinction between us at college—
veterans and non-veterans—grew out of the general
knowledge that, overwhelmingly, those of us who
served were draftees. There were some who, the day

after Pearl Harbor, had stepped forward, volunteering for duty (young George Bush was one of them). Probably by the time I was old enough, several years into the war, I'd have volunteered. I suppose so—the Second World War, unlike its two successors in Korea and Vietnam, having been a relatively popular war, causing the patriotic juices to run. But one never knew; so that as the differences betwen the six hundred and the twelve hundred crystallized, all that was detectable was the faint air of urgency characterizing a young man older by several years than he'd have been if he had gone right to college from high school. The day I matriculated at Yale, I was older than my older brother Jim when he graduated from Yale—to be sure, under the pressure of an accelerated academic schedule brought on by Pearl Harbor.

But that sense of time lost—in the case of some of my classmates as much as three years, and even four in a few cases—brought on dead-seriousness in the matter of getting on, with both academic life and extra-academic life. A married Yale undergraduate before the war was a phenomenon, someone to stare at. By senior year, three of my closest friends had been married. One dashing classmate, before matriculation, had not only been married, but divorced, soon after which he married for the second time. The faculty remarked on the intensity with which we tended to take our classes. Probably the veterans and the non-veterans consumed, per capita, about the same amount of booze. But for the veterans, it was simply more of what they had been doing for several years; the younger students were going through the anarchic throes of animal-house roistering. In general, we veterans were simply—busy. Life and its priorities were more focused. I remember being told with amusement several years after the event that when he had solemnly informed me of the date and hour at which I should report, with other members of my delegation, to be formally initiated into our fraternity, I had appalled my sponsor, an upperclassman but a non-veteran, younger than I, by telling him offhandedly that I was not available at that particular hour as I had an assignment to do for the student newspaper. He was apparently too shocked to remonstrate.

As I reflect back on the scene forty years later, I think I would not find many classmates who disagreed with this finding, namely that those of us who were involved in the war felt a certain affinity for one another. Hard to define (nothing is "impossible" to define, Mr. Ross of *The New Yorker* was telling us about that time); limited, greatly attenuated; but the bond was there, and if I am not mistaken it is still there. I must suppose that that bond cannot compare in its reality or intensity with that shared, say, by fellow members of the Peace Corps, let alone by Mormon missionaries who, as young people, did extensive work.

I think, then, of the great centrifugal factors of
modern life, and again for maximum reliability stay
in the autobiographical mode. I write these words late
at night in the garage-study of my home, a house occupied by me and my wife for almost forty years. I have
twice laid eyes on the neighbor north of my property,
and I have yet to lay eyes on my neighbor to the south,
who has occupied the house for fifteen years. By tem-
perament I was readily convinced of the plausibility of
what was widely considered an idiosyncrasy of its author, namely that good fences make good neighbors.
But even good fences are permeable, and mine do not
tend to be; and, I suspect, it is so with many Americans,
who feel a growing isolation from one another. Even
if we grant that there are always natural magnets of
social gravitation—race, religion, geographical propin-
quity, shared college experience—all of these when
alive, even when vibrant, do less than bring on that
pulsation of consanguinity that makes the resident of
Florida feel as genuinely as he might his bonds to the
Hawaiian beachcomber, or the Laramie cowboy, or
the college-campus litterateur in Greenwich Village.
In a once-famous introduction to his book on the phenomenon of post-Stalin-Hitler-pact France, Anton
Rossi recited a conversation between strangers at a
coffeehouse in Paris which went something like this,
one middle-aged man suddenly accosting the elderly

stranger at the adjacent table, both with newspapers
in hand, both bent double before their demitasses.

"Excuse me, but do you like Jews?"

"No."

"Well, do you like Catholics?"

"No."

"Well, do you like Americans?"

"No."

"British?"

"No."

"Well. Whom *do* you like?"

"I like my friends." The elderly man resumes
reading his paper.

I am not conversant with the literature of clinical
psychology, and do not intend to become so. But I sense
intuitively that while friendship does not necessarily
grow out of experience shared, experience shared con-
duces to a bond from which friendship can grow. I
move on to say that my conviction is that friendship is
strengthened by such experiences as bring out in us
that which ever so lightly elevates us from the trough
of self-concern and self-devotion. There has got to be
a reason why, at public spectacles, one applauds the
hero or sympathizes with the victim. I cannot help but
conclude that to seek to activate in each of us impulses
which are most often there will give more of us the

opportunity to see, in ourselves and in each other, what otherwise we'd be less likely to see. And to heighten the prospect that, as citizens of a country we achingly long to make as great as the legends insist that the United States is, we will be venerating the real thing.

A P P E N D I X

☆ ☆ ☆ ☆ ☆ ☆ ☆ ☆ ☆ ☆ ☆

THE COSTS AND DISTRIBUTION OF FEDERAL AID, FY 1988
(States Ranked on 1988 Per Capita Incomes)

State	Per Capita Income, 1988 Rank	Amount	% of Total Federal Taxes	Federal Grants (a)	Federal Taxes Per $1.00 of Federal Grants (b)
Conn.	1	$22,761	2.03%	1.42%	$1.43
D.C.		21,667	0.35	1.49	0.23
N.J.	2	21,882	4.58	3.06	1.50
Mass.	3	20,701	3.10	3.06	1.01
Alas.	4	19,514	0.26	0.53	0.49
Md.	5	19,314	2.24	1.84	1.22
N.Y.	6	19,299	8.81	11.51	0.77
N.H.	7	19,016	0.53	0.37	1.43
Cal.	8	18,855	12.81	10.67	1.20
Del.	9	17,699	0.32	0.29	1.10
Va.	10	17,640	2.54	1.80	1.41
Ill.	11	17,611	5.23	4.29	1.22
Nev.	12	17,440	0.45	0.30	1.50
Ha.	13	16,898	0.42	0.44	0.95

| State | Per Capita Income, 1988 | | % of Total | | Federal Taxes Per $1.00 of |
	Rank	Amount	Federal Taxes	Federal Grants (a)	Federal Grants (b)
R.I.	14	16,793	0.43	0.59	0.73
Minn.	15	16,787	1.78	1.95	0.91
Wash.	16	16,569	1.86	1.96	0.95
Fla.	17	16,546	5.17	3.14	1.65

17 Above
Average States: $18,459   52.56%   47.22% $1.11

(AVERAGE PER CAPITA INCOME, U.S. POPULATION, $16,444)

Col.	18	16,417	1.31	1.10	1.19
Mich.	19	16,387	3.86	3.90	0.99
Pa.	20	16,168	4.85	5.35	0.91
Kan.	21	15,905	0.95	0.80	1.19
Mo.	22	15,492	1.96	1.78	1.10
Oh.	23	15,485	4.20	4.32	0.97
Wis.	24	15,444	1.80	2.05	0.88
Vt.	25	15,382	0.20	0.30	0.67
Neb.	26	15,184	0.56	0.65	0.86
Ore.	27	14,982	0.98	1.02	0.96
Ga.	28	14,980	2.29	2.72	0.84
Me.	29	14,976	0.42	0.61	0.69
Ariz.	30	14,887	1.24	1.07	1.16
Ia.	31	14,764	0.97	1.10	0.88
Ind.	32	14,721	1.99	1.80	1.11
Tex.	33	14,640	6.20	4.72	1.31
N.C.	34	14,128	2.19	2.11	1.04
Wy.	35	13,718	0.16	0.25	0.64
Tenn.	36	13,659	1.64	1.92	0.85

State	Per Capita Income, 1988		% of Total		Federal Taxes Per $1.00 of
State	Rank	Amount	Federal Taxes	Federal Grants (a)	Federal Grants (b)
Okla.	37	13,269	1.04	1.29	0.81
Ky.	38	12,795	1.10	1.61	0.68
S.C.	39	12,764	1.03	1.24	0.83
N.D.	40	12,720	0.22	0.42	0.52
Mon.	41	12,670	0.24	0.46	0.52
Ida.	42	12,657	0.29	0.42	0.69
Ala.	43	12,604	1.22	1.53	0.80
N.M.	44	12,481	0.44	0.67	0.66
S.D.	45	12,475	0.21	0.40	0.53
La.	46	12,193	1.27	1.96	0.65
Ark.	47	12,172	0.66	0.92	0.72
Ut.	48	12,013	0.46	0.63	0.73
W.Va.	49	11,658	0.51	0.97	0.53
Miss.	50	10,992	0.63	1.20	0.53
33 Below Average States:		$13,963	47.09%	51.29%	$0.92
Memo:					
5 Richest States		$20,834	12.21%	9.91%	$1.23
5 Poorest States		11,806	3.53	5.68	0.62

a. Excludes payments in lieu of taxes and shared revenues.
b. Estimated by dividing the percent of federal taxes paid, by state, by the percent of federal grants received.

Source: Department of Commerce (per capita income); Tax Foundation (tax and grant distributions).

INDEX
OF NAMES AND
SELECTED TOPICS

☆ ☆ ☆ ☆ ☆ ☆ ☆ ☆ ☆ ☆ ☆

About the Author

WILLIAM F. BUCKLEY, JR., did national service in the Army of the United States during World War II. He is variously credited with trying to show New York voters what needs to be done for their city, and with transforming the conservative movement in the United States. His own keenly thought-through and deeply felt political convictions have never prevented him from scrutinizing different points of view and giving them ventilation. From his first notable and provocative book, *God and Man at Yale*, Bill Buckley has gone on to lecture and teach, to preside over his long-lasting television program, *Firing Line*, and to write essays, widely syndicated columns, and analytical and biographical nonfiction that has won wide praise. He has been called "the conservative master of the well-made argument" (*Publishers Weekly*), and "modern American conservatism's great teacher" (*The Washington Times*). He also writes a series of best-selling thrillers featuring one Blackford Oakes, a character who does his duty and repays his patrimony by sustained service, often at great personal risk, in the Central Intelligence Agency.

The Buckleys' home is in Stamford, Connecticut.